GLOBALISATION

The Sphere Keeps Spinning
A Poetry Anthology

COMPILED BY
KELLY VAN NELSON

MMH PRESS

First published in Australia in 2021
by MMH Press
Waikiki, WA 6169

Interior design by: Dylan Ingram
Cover design by: Chelsea Wilcox

NATIONAL LIBRARY OF AUSTRALIA

A catalogue record for this work is available from the National Library of Australia

National Library of Australia Catalogue-in-Publication data:
Globalisation/Kelly Van Nelson

ISBN: 978-0-6450966-1-3
(Paperback)

ISBN: 978-0-6450966-2-0
(eBook)

Introduction

I have always been a poet. Someone searching for the right words to express emotions that otherwise have no rhyme or reason. From my journey as a lost child to an adult misfit, poetry was always the creative outlet that gave me a vehicle to channel good and bad energy. Being an author was once a lonely profession, one with long stretches spent filling the page with meaningful words and nights editing and reformatting a piece so it could give emphasis where most needed and hold space in the right places. It was a silent world that existed only in my imagination and in the eyes of my readers.

then
the
pandemic
came

With its wrath came lockdowns. Periods of lengthy isolation separated people from loved ones and could so easily have brought humanity to its knees. Yet amidst the chaos and uncertainty, poets around the world found one another. I attended my first online zoom open mic event when I was the middle of stay at home orders in Sydney, Australia during the first wave of COVID. I spotted an event on Facebook inviting poets of all levels to tune in and share work in a safe and friendly environment. I connected that day and listened to a stream of emerging and established artists recite material that blew me away. I took a deep breath, shared one or two of my own poems, and was hooked. Over the last year, I've had long bouts of separation from my husband who has been quarantined more times than I can count on my hands due to working interstate and the border challenges here in

Australia. So, I embraced the virtual poetry scene to keep myself sane. Some weekends, I travelled via Zoom to five countries in one day, from Australia and New Zealand, across Asia, to the UK or the USA. I pulled all-nighters visiting poetry events in every Australian state, popped in for a brew and a few verses in Nashville, Aberdeen, London, Paris, and Singapore, hung out with the midnight poets who never slept. During a brainstorming session with my publisher, Karen Mc Dermott, we formulated a plan to launch our own Australian open mic event, hosted monthly by myself and Melbourne poet, Tanya Southey. Making Magic Happen Press Poetry Night has gone from strength to strength, showcasing a live event streamed in the 2020 Melbourne Fringe Festival with talent poets from around the world performing their best work. To collaborate with Making Magic Happen Press on this project, to capture some of the work from these incredible poets in an anthology, is a dream come true. This is our time to bask in the sunlight.

I have been moved to tears listening to the trauma of friends in this welcoming community of diverse artists, healing their wounds on the open mic. Laughter has been a gift from the satire poets who deliver impromptu lines packed with insights into our own absurdities. Friendship has formed with people met only on screen, yet they provide the shoulder to absorb tears and an ear for listening to the deepest secrets of our turbulent pasts. Respect glued together this group from different generations, raised with varied social backgrounds and upbringings. Inclusiveness has woven magical tentacles through separate lives, bringing us together in a sea of colourful life. We found our true selves in words written from alternative perspectives, showcasing a writing form like no other that offers a coping mechanism for the angst of loss, the confusion of a viral outbeak, and the disbelief at our own disrespect of the planet we inhabit as visitors passing through only for a short while. Our poems capture forever an era where resilience, humility, and empathy bring us to a place of strength. A timeless moment in history when a president is sworn in by a poet laureate and the spoken word has its own viral outbreak. There is no cure for poetry. Only infectious passion for those who choose to embrace its powers.

To all the poets who contributed to this anthology, we have been through so much together, sharing our problems and spreading life's joys, free of judgement, always wrapping our arms around one another in unconditional support and love.

We are family.

Kelly

xxx

Contents

VIRAL OUTBREAK

CONSUMED

MOTHER NATURE

FOUND IN SPACE

LOST ON EARTH

Four Seasons In One Day
Kelly Van Nelson

Brittle autumn leaves
crunch underfoot as we tread
carefully, afraid

winter is coming,
bringing in lethal virus
amidst cruel snowstorm

taking spring from step
as we backtrack to a time
when cure evades thee

and impatiently
we pray for summer sunrise —
hope on horizon-

Gone

Fraser Gordon

Silent, alone, watched with sadness
Immersed in sorrow with focussed breath
I retrace beautiful heart crushing steps
Each fractured memory, vividly blurred
Regret, loss, regret, loss, rewind, repeat
She rests, not me
No such sombre joy will I endure
Just emptiness
Never to be filled

Man On A Mountain

Fin Hall

Man on a mountain
Sitting very still
Keeping away from heartache
Keeping away from romance
Keeping away from the big city developers
Tearing down the past
Envisage now, this solitary figure
The expression on his face
Is he lonely?
Is he sad?
Is he deaf to the outside world?
Is he shedding a tear for all the things he has left behind?
The man on a mountain
Is glad
No more false bravados
No more drunken blurs
No more consternation
No more childish arguments in childish situations.
Man on a mountain
Sitting now at peace
No bowing down to the taxman
No bowing down to bureaucracy
No bowing down to fools
No bowing down to anyone because
Now, he is nobody's tool
His thoughts,
"You can't fool me
You can't fool me with your brilliant talk
You can't fool me.
I could run before I could walk
I know what's happening
I know exactly what you're trying to do
You can't pull the wool over my eyes
I can see right through you
No fancy explanations
I can beat you at your game
I am sure footed
You're not dealing with the tame.
I'm wild

I can read your every thought
I'm no child
I won't get caught
I know what you're trying to do
You can't fool me."
His words
His words to you
"You can't help if you're really stupid
Believe you me, you don't have to prove it
You can't help if you're stupid, can you?
It's not your fault if you appear really thick
Or if you're so bad, you make me sick
It's not my fault either,
is it?
So just go, and leave me alone,
Why don't you stay in your home
And stop
Just stop
And leave me on my mountain."

A Shoe In

Kristy-Lee Swift

I walked around the globe complete.
I tripped up on my own two feet.
Then hobbled all the way back home with something stuck inside my shoe.
That something was an ism; I'd collected quite a few.
There was sex, race and material, trans-gender, fundamental,
Politic and global and hundreds more for all I knew.
Once home, I took my shoes off to my mother's great distress,
I tipped out a mob of isms, a pile of sand, and then, I left.
Barefoot, I took off to the beach and swam with nothing on.
That nothing was a joy to wear although I wished I'd brought my thongs.
Only since those isms I'd collected and brought home
Had poked into my feet as long 'round the globe I'd roamed.
Those things, they must be sharp of tooth, I figured, took my flesh for meat,
Really that's all that it is but, sure, the thought is none too sweet.
Salt water stung the open wounds but does speed up the healing.
You need that when it's with those isms, so long, you've been dealing.
I see you're dealing none too well with isms and it's telling.
Though, unsure to whom I'm speaking, I am thus inclined, into the blue, to yelling.
Though, it should explain the reason that I stand, barefoot in sand
Seeming somewhat out of mind and shouting t'ward both sea and land.
Mostly it's the doubting and the wondering, without clue
Why those isms want to travel here. And, why by shoe?
I limped back home, full of intent on asking all those isms
Just to ask a thing or two of how they make decisions
But first I'd best refine my questions, and I'll do that…soon
Must be careful not to upset isms lest Mum might fetch the wooden spoon.
She'd chase me with that rotten thing and scoop up all my isms
Pop them in a nice safe box and tape it, labelled what it's not,
And you know what? I bet you do, the next time I go looking,
"Where are they?" I would plead but her reply, "I just forgot".
She'd put them in a safe, safe place, all neatly packed away
And in that place, like all forgotten things, they safely stay.
Until, by happy accident, I'd trip over the box.
My knee'd be skinned from tripping and I'd upset the lazy lot, but hey,
The isms, bleary-eyed and cross, would slowly and with caution creep out from their safety box.
They'd rub their eyes and give a cough and one would turn to say,
Yes, one would seem about to speak; its index finger raised,

A drawn in breath and flash of teeth, but all I'd hear is: Squeak, squeak, squeak.
The squeaking, though impassioned, I'd be forced to realise
I'd never comprehend and there would be no compromise.
For I don't speak squeak, and even more, I don't intend on learning,
Even more, what isms had to say seemed less and less concerning
For they had nibbled on my feet, and yet, I'd had my questions written
Mum, however, made my questions neat so they'd go missin'
So, I vacuumed up the sandy pile then tidied up the whole damn place.
I made sure the isms were all neatly tucked into their little space.
No questions asked or answered, next I dumped the vacuum dust outside
Amongst some rocks my mother loved and had displayed with pride.
The rocks had come in boxes. Mother found them at the shops,
Gave me the task of painting them as pretty kindness rocks
I remembered having wondered if on one or maybe two
If anyone would notice something different, only on a few
Instead, adorned with something else, with something I preferred.
Something sharp and witty or compellingly absurd.
I foraged through the kindness, searching for just one,
Just one of my wits would serve me well though I found none.
Only kindness rocks were left and what good were they to anyone
"If it brings a smile, it's worthwhile," or so my mother said
I took to throwing kindness rocks at all the passers by
But no one ever smiled and I made a baby cry
The final kindness rock I hurled, it whacked some poor guy right in the head
The ambulance took way too long and so the guy was dead
I'd have gone to that guy's funeral saying sorry for the stoning
"I didn't mean to harm the guy," I'd planned to say to those who'd known him.
But as those words went 'round my head, I couldn't help but giggle.
So instead of that guy's funeral, at Mother's curt request,
I dutifully brushed hair and teeth and dutifully skipped to bed.
And there I kept on giggling 'till my mother made a call.
"My child is gone mad," she cried. And so what followed was my fall.
My mother fetched my father's gun then stood me up against a wall.
She fired off some shots. I fell. And, so her job was done.
My mother left the call; she Zooms and Facetimes so that's how you word it.
You don't hang up, instead, just leave, without goodbyes or quick reprieve
Not that I could have heard it.

Journeys
Maroulla Radisavic

Removing the mask! Who are you?
I don't talk to strangers.
Who am I? I lost my identity.
I remember it. Please give it back to me.
What's my date of birth?
Country of origin?
What's my religion?
What's my tradition?
Who are you? Who am I?
We're all equal, but are we the same?
Are we all numbers?
We're all a clay toy behind a mask.
Countless cultures lost in space.
The globe is a beautiful place.
Where is it?
Why can't we be ourselves?
I want my language back.
I have a story to tell.
Ask me.
It's a long story.
I will tell you.
Please ask me.
I am an individual behind the mask.
You are a toy made of clay.
You came from the womb of the earth
You cannot kill your mother.
(In her dreams)—who are you?
I'm your mother…
But where do you live?
We're in 252bc
One-way train ticket…
I was the image, I was the character
Sell me weapons
I can sell them Peace
Sell me at high prices
I sell them for free
Sell me war
I sell them flowers
Fairies and witches…
Kings and dragons…
Looked death in the face…
Journeys…
Diving in.

Erasure
Imogen Arate

To them, I am white
My paleness fails
to escape categorization

Across this pond
suddenly I'm given elevation
outgrowing the frame
of the "forever immigrant"

Back home
where I must be the foreigner
cast to tell stories
of ancestors from exotic lands

Stuck on repeat
on grooves cut at the base
of the Himalayas
and just as deadly
when I attempt to scale

to stand tall on my own two feet

to escape mental barriers
set more firmly than those peaks

Your Shit Is Our Shit

Phil Saunders

the world
and our corner of it
can be a great place
but sometimes
a lot of s**t happens
all at once
and covers us
with sadness

tears sit
close beneath
on my your our world

we are but strangers
travelling through
bouncing, slipping, sliding
against our neighbours
(fellow) travellers all

no excuses

Survival Of The Thinkiest
Bryan Franco

I come from a place
where selfishness
is synonymous with survival.

It is not uncommon for me
to traverse knee deep snow
when getting out of bed
on sweltering summer days.
And despite that
I am numb knee to ankle,
the soles of my feet burn
from scorching summer sand.
There are people
who claim
to feel no pain
when walking barefoot
over hot coals.
Welcome to the world
of mind over matter
where people feel no pain,
but their feet
are bloodied and blistered.

I come from a place
where selfishness
is synonymous with survival:
where success
cannot happen without sacrifice.

I come from a place called Earth:
a giant ball
of dirt, stone, water and gasses
littered with plants and animals.
Amongst the animals
is a creature called human.
Unlike like the rest
who simply survive,
humans think;
humans reason;
humans justify

There are over seven billion humans
scurrying about
trying to find their place
on this place called Earth.
If one of these
thinking, reasoning, justifying creatures
truly found its place,
it could stay put.
but we all have to move
to get out of bed.

Patriarchal Poison

Yola Bakker

Oh the irony
Soul of a man
Who I adore so
All of you I feel
I see you.

Posers on podiums and pedestals
Just how far this patriarch's poisonous paradigm
Hurts every woman we all know
But look how it destroys the gentle man's tender divine
I see you.

Born to a mother
Soft nurtured nature
Into a chest thumping construct
Of alphas to whom you do not relate
I see you.

Drawn to safe havens which skim
Surface sale fixes of "I'll take care of you"
Masculinity maverick's unacknowledged shame
Bitterness barricades a baffling brew
I see you.

To salvage senses of stillness in belonging
Within an insidious ecosystem
Where toxicity tempers purity of all human kind
Our paths crossed for a reason
I see you.

Fundamental co-dependency
Sheer extent of our environment's sick mask
Victims to our surroundings which sell souls
We are but acrimonious ants marching along dead logs riddled with rot
I see you.

Isolated in careers, cars, cafes and shops
Isolated at traffic lights these never ending pit stops
Isolated in our neighbourhoods we're taught to believe
Isolated is normal get on with the grieve
I see you.

Distinguish between your resistance to the fall and your actual fall
To all the dark daimon beauty has to offer in its infinite wisdom
I see you.

Distinguish between the unaware woman that disempowers you
by indulging the addictions of a sickness labelled yours
And the woman that treats you as an equal
by calling out a sickness which is not at all yours but in fact ours
I see you.

Congestion by constant calibrations of cunning constraints
The need to keep relationships calm and ordered
Is a highly specialised form of suffering that fails to see the fine line that separates
That which simmers from the screams of shackled servitude
And alas for which your free spirit was born
that being the sophistication of sustainable service
I see you.

Oh the irony
Soul of a man
Who I adore so
All of you I feel
I see you.

Travel With A Coward's Heart

Angela Costi

As I walked from the adobe house to the welded gate
enclosing an ancient chorus of forced starvation,
described as a 'Tucson garden',
I ingested the penetrating stares
of the saguaro cacti,
their shadows cast a march of giants
who swallowed my attempt to lean with my chest.

It may have been the silence of those guns
hanging from the porches like Christmas baubles,
the sinister shutters closing their eyes,
the thud of ghost cowboy boots –
a spook circled my vertebrae
smoking the cigar of untimely death.

I thought I mastered the language of listen,
knew how to inhale difference better than air,
between rib cage and breastbone
I had the happy lumps of adventures
circa 1991
on a motorbike speeding through New Delhi,
trekking the Annapurna and sleeping among
constellations of accent and dialect.

Thirty years later, 'warning' stitches my skin,
nerves of ancestral wars quilted to bones of daily news,
alarms, alerts, rations, curfews…
these threads twist into narrative and history,
into a rush to retrace my steps.

Inside

Fraser Gordon

Four walls, bleak and devoid of character
My only sanctuary from the inside outside of this new world

Scheduled fun, well intended to maintain a grip on reality
Has the unintended effect of quite the opposite

Clocks tick, locked up slower than outside
Trapped and scared like some baited beast
I claw at the doors I see, and those I can't

New friends, not friends share their sadness
Is this me. Am I them?

Share, talk, search, confide
Trying to trick them with regurgitated normalcy

First time I get a brief respite, joy is replaced almost instantly
by fear as anxiety crushes my lungs until I cannot breathe
The comfort of going "home",
not home but now home brings short lived relief which quickly pales

Alone and afraid, nowhere is safe now.

A Glut Of Words
Denise O'hagan

'The limits of my language means the limits of my universe.'
– Ludwig Wittgenstein

On any given day
There is a glut of words around me
On doorways, streets and signs
Informing, instructing, warning
On labels, shops and cars
Coaxing, cajoling, luring
In restaurants and bars
The many-tentacled monster
Of modern communication
Pressing in around me,
Assertive and insistent
Audacious and capricious
Oppressing and compressing me
Sometimes, they almost make me choke.
But then there are others
The passed over or forgotten words
Scrawled on beggars' placards
The bewildered words
Whispered away in the slipstream of time
Crumpled thoughts in a lover's thrown-away note
Fragments of people's conversations
Caught in the wind on a street corner.

Must it be like this?
Words should be held like little gems
Precious-like
In the soft cup of a child's hand
And picked out tenderly, one by one
So we can slip into the lining of situations
And see them from the inside.

Originally published in *Scarlet Leaf Review*, 21 January 2019

I Am The Speck In The Globe
Rosa Carrafa

Eyes look at me.
They do not see me.
Hands touch me.
They do not feel me.
Words are spoken at me.
But not to me.
I get forgotten.
But remembered when you have the need.
You invited me.
But only once you were reminded of me.
You ask me in a hurry 'How are you?'
But not talk with me to ask me 'How I am feeling?'
This world has always been too big for me,
For little me gets lost among the development that is structured and uniform.
Perhaps your world is not the same as mine,
For I get lost among the global immensity of it all.
It may be globalization for some,
But for little me, I ask:
'Who has the eyes on me?'
'Whose hands touch me?'
'Who will speak to me?'
'Why the last minute invite?'
'Why do I receive the passing ask of how I am?'
All of this is a globe of loneliness,
I am real enough to know the difference between being alone and feeling lonely,
I am the little speck in the globe that moves in my own way.
Not as the globe wants me.
This is the reality of the speck of human cells that make up me.
I am not here to be popular,
Who is the speck in the globe?
I am.

Not My War
Julia Kaylock

So many angry people
Trouble everywhere
Voiceless people shouting
Into vacant air
Desperate, disenfranchised,
Wanting to be heard
Their best is just not good enough
No power in their words.
I have no answer for their plight
I can't conceive their need to fight
I'm only grateful that I'm white
And dark despair is something
That I cannot begin to write.

"America the beautiful"
Some sang in cloistered halls
But now the truth is manifest
They're breaking down the walls,
Martin Luther King Junior
Once advocated peace
His words, though sage on history's page
Can't help the people find release.
So now, from where I sit and stare
At what is happening over there
I'm choosing to refuse to see
Oppression
        exists
            everywhere.

The Long Game
Megan Chapman

Life is a long game.
My life is my long game.

I've been trapped in
this fog of angst
For I don't know how long,
the days dropping
one after the other,
sameness belied only by a name,
beginnings and endings lost
in the endless morphing
of evenings and mornings
"And the evening and the morning were the (next) day"

But there are questions,
Always an infinite variety of questions,
each as individual
and unique as a fingerprint,
each formed
to further our own singular quest,
to make sense of
this overwhelm.

What day is this?
When will it end?
How will it end?
Why am I here?
What is it all about anyway?
What do I do now?

Answering is a choice,
and how I answer
colours all that follows.
How is it that my answers
make meaning
and bring value to
each minute detail
of the minutes
that translate into the procession of hours
And days and weeks and years
Of my life?

Does this current state of flux
Determine how I move through it,
Or do I?
Do I choose to be the governor of my life,
the arbiter of my fate?
Or,
Shall I just drift
Seeing only past and no future,
Oblivious to the power I have
in how I choose to spend the now.

Do I ask the questions
And make my choices,
Or,
do I simply succumb to the seduction
Of the comfort
of a familiar discomfort that seems
just too hard to swim against?

Riding the riptide of revelations
Is too exhausting.
It's easier to just avoid some answers -
Put them in the 'Too Hard basket'
The 'I'll get back to it' pile
The 'I want to be the grasshopper singing all summer I don't care if I starve in the winter' category.
Free and wild.
No care for consequences.

Life is a long game.
If my life is my long game,
In this infinite continuum of beginnings and endings,
There's never a time when I can have failed -
There's always another question to be answered,
Another experiment to be run.
An alternative strategy to be tried.

Life is a long game.
It's THE long game.

Somewhere Overseas

Angela Costi

There is a woman in a bedsit
six flights, fourteenth door
living in silence she writes:
'if my world is my thoughts on paper
then contentment is surely accessible.'
Split curtain exposes
the same sky for the next woman
in the makeshift canopy of crestfallen dresses
twisted to earth like sandbags in trenches
she writes:
'but contentment is a greater place
than a hometown
and world-knowledge should be
a first-hand experience.'
Looking up
at the bang of blue
shared with the next woman
in the steel bar basement,
a concrete pillow to bed her diary
she writes: 'the emphasis of experience
is what I need to convince people.'
The clouds tumble in a wake of shadows
for the next woman
with a bay-view alcove of manicured roses
who writes:
'to convince myself of my own validity
is the greatest battle.'

The Perpetual Manifesto
Gerard Traub

Hurled into the world's immensity
with great sweeps of madness
striking unfathomable reservoirs
until lost amidst this pervading darkness.

To exalt the monster at the helm
the masses excited by pleasure and revolt
applauding campaigns of aggression
upon our feverish and perilous march.

Through anxious and calculating eyes
forging will to power and violent assault
to pale the miraculous so finite
exploring the many gestures of war
with a sleepless and magnified rationale.

Here to break forth from every husk
into the summit of this maelstrom
a contempt which orders all of nature
to cower and fall before us
plunged into a ruthless splendour
where any dreams are vanquished
left choking inside our glorified mausoleums.

How we clutch the air with predatory fire
struggle to kill the stillness of fragile skies
launching our relentless and insolent challenge
until cowered under this trembling age.

World Domination

Dane Ince

When I was growing up the only thing I wanted to be was me
They tried to beat the shape out of me
I just kept coming back for more
No idea why
Not able to ascertain when enough was enough
Or my will to have get what I want was stronger than theirs to beat me
After a while they gave out gave up all worn out
Probably about the time I learned to lie
Yeah that did it
In the end they failed
They beat the shape right into me deep inside instead of out
Contrariwise to the plan to goal
Folded hands closed polite and quiet
Beat it really deep
With a bullwhip from Mexico
A fist to the face
Beaten that shape so far down now it's just a shake
Now it's just a knee jerk reaction to the plans of the cult for world domination.

Em Ontvlecetv / Invaded

Dr. Deidra Suwanee Dees

you invaded my space with anti-climactic explosion,
you purged my tongue with a new breed of speech,
Vhopvketv Muscogee values descend upon erosion,
how can you still drive me into retreat?

your support for Jews in the great holocaust
makes me want to believe you hold empathy,
Opunvkv my Indigenous language is almost lost,
why can't I convince you to believe in me?

when Muscogees ruled, we had enough to eat,
children went to sleep at night in a safe place,
Enokketv there were no deadly police nor COVID disease,
but now you behold an emaciated race;

vanishing ancestral land that belonged to me,
I am the essence of a dying turtle's call,
Asomkita you've stolen everything—*even my dignity,*
how can you hurt me more when i've already lost it all?

Close Encounters
Daragh Byrne

A walk in my home village
is the slow murder of intimacies
that I ran from. I'm jetlagged,
catching my mother up
on another year's indecencies.
You'd swear it was her that was
prodigal; her local criticality is
manifest in pavement meetings
ordained by chance's fancy.
We're pecked by stop-and-chats,
all wink and elbow knowingness —
the sort of cheap and easy talk
that has the heft of hearth
and haven.
                    A week before,
ten thousand miles away,
in Westfield, Bondi Junction,
I ran into my sister, shopping.
Later by the beach at Bronte,
a friend out walking called my name.
Love is made from happenstance
at each end of the globe;
close encounters seal the distance
in ways that leave no telling
which part of me is truly home.

Fragilities Fail

Yola Bakker

A dime a dreary dozen
Following the flow with fantasies of being "in-flow"
Unaware just how untouched you are by alternate worlds
As you hover in hiding behind all you benefit from
Quick to cast and quiet to call
Slow to stand and sanctimonious to fall
Wallow in the fragility of your shallow comfort
Unaware of the disdain that you breed
And the damage you dictate each drive
As your frivolous fain forges falseness and fakery

Boob jobs before bearing babies
Chronic callous cries before beads of sacred sweat
Performance pieces by puppets upstaging truthful transcendence
Big toys and lavish houses of empty exaggerations eager for endorsement
How materialism coarsens the spirit as you stray further still from the crucial concrete diagnosis that is yours

Dramatic defensive devices
Precious princess pretentiousness
Death by deceitful debt

A flat undisturbed life doesn't reveal the illuminance of human existence
Nor bring about the being's highest value
Rather here your ordinary intelligence stagnates
Respect beyond mere understanding for soul's culture over heroic credentials
Problems are not absent of meaning as your blindness and deafness to it will have you believe
Seeing beauty through selfless self-absorption ultimate reprieve

Even as you read this your attention and focus will scatter
Gripped by a lust for validation from vacant vessels
By sheer incapacity to allow beauty to stir your soul out of its static slumber
In avid attempts to avoid painful presentations of life
Offering deep revelations missed by the spoilt lens of your egocentric eyes
An invisible radiance for all that is exponential in depth and meaning
At risk of forever being lost

To Tell

Riya Rajesh

"my inside likes it but my outside doesn't"
says my seven year old sister
as if it is normal to have
two selves sown
together in one body
outside girl singing loud,
belting new and newer sounds
inside girl's quiet hum
her whisper
her blurred
s_lho_ette
gaps in her form
muffled and bound
lips zipped
together but still she hums

my words could belong to so many stories
humming women who are not me
who have neither my privilege nor my ache
beaks long
longing bodies arched toward the skies

but today my words belong to my sister,
my seven year old wonder
who definitely sees colour
my sister who does not want the other kids to sound
out
her full name
permanent marker on her lunch bag
still learning to meld
constantly turning,
my acrobat

i want to tell
her, she does not have to tear or be torn
even if
humming is all she is allowed or
allows herself
i want to tell
her, even as i
delete ~~tamil songs~~ from my search
history

Begin/End

Claire Language

In the beginning, there were lots of tales. There were all these half-spun trails where we kinda met. I remember being really scared of you, I think, because the warmth felt so different to my skin and the days curled so nicely like I had only been born once before. They all said, there is a beast, somewhere there, and I believed them. You can't not be angry with a mind like that.

Fire was probably my best friend at that time, you cut my hair and I cut yours. We looked the same. But I breathed differently. And you could split open the sky with your finger, touch it with your lips, delightful nakedness.

Somewhere before the sky is deep green, and before I [screamed] at any gaping hole of mirrors. We were animals, deep and dark and ravenous and whole. Times that looped like rhythms, like maybe we were sick of it? Like maybe we got sick of it. Little sweet angel belle, where did you go? Afternoon cruising drunk drivers, like cups overflowing, like skin overbearing. I break a plate and then make it mosaic. So, we weren't so bad after all?

I Only Knew Her As My Wife
Imogen Arate

She came into my life with a full suitcase
A couch-surfing ad I placed caught her attention
her ingenuity and artistry caught mine
A three-night stay elongated into months

She would introduce me to her family
Though her father and I were divided by language
we shared a love of photography
He had a vintage analog Nikon
whose viewfinder he loved to peer through
while gleefully winding the film
with its tiny lever before clicking
on the button just to its left
then peak his face from behind the lens
grinning ear to ear
It was a love that we understood
without the need for a translator

She stockpiled handmade wallpaper
on the rack I built for her in the backyard
We talked about the projects she had planned
the collages that would reflect her experiences in life
My workdays would end with her stories
of discovery in daily field trips
offering fresh insight into this neighborhood
I had called home my entire life

One day her visa expired
the next I saw the tan silhouette
of her a-line trench sashay away
I was meant to follow
Work emergencies got in the way
then concerns about my adjustment
to a foreign life
and excuses and fears stretched
the band of time

The declaration of war came
I forget when
It was a blur
of political intrigue and lies for gain

But I became an officer
and the tides of invasion
washed me onto her shores

Salted only by the stench of war
I made my way to their home
hoping to shield them
from a known dreaded fate
Covered in the dust of debris
I stumbled passed
mounts of withered flesh
liquefying in a stale stew
of iron and cabbage
under the judgmental glare
of an unforgiving sun

A door covered in patterns
recalling her old adventures
easily gave way
to an unexpected greeting
Her father pointed his Nikon
my way to shoot
and I convulsed
at the shutter's clacking

He peaked his familiar
smiling face
then pulled out the film
falling into a limp pile beside him
like the hope for a reconciliation
between our two nations

We then both got on our knees
to creep toward her who
lay weeping in our midst
A pocket knife I pulled out
while he undressed her
top half yet still covered
and I sawed into her wrist
while explaining that
this was the only prevention

to save her body from being sullied
when the ensuing troops came

You Never Arrived (The Ghosts Of Calais)

Des Mannay

Avoid the trap
of vengeance -
turning on us
when Terrorists massacre kids.
We ran away from men who plant bombs,
wield guns - demand absolute power -
our enemies too.
Why we are here.
If I had not left Syria I would have died.
If I stay in "the jungle" over winter I could die too
in a donated tent.
Easy tinder for a tarpaulin Kristallnacht.
Bonfires of hatred.
We came to Europe to find the land of human rights.
Instead we are left here in this camp.
Even asylum seekers.
If we could get a proper roof we would stay.
No solution
here in this hell hole.
We must escape from this place.
Higher fences/more cops
make it harder to leave.
Borders are too strong.
Death returns -
a Syrian run over on the motorway
in front of her son,
an Afghan boy hit by a train.
I join the protests on the roundabout -
"Open the borders!".
My friend lives in hope
he'll make it to Britain.
Has relatives there.
Others pray for salvation.
I will no longer pray for myself ...
I've seen newspapers visitors bring -
dead babies washed up on the shore.
I fall on my knees.
Prostrate myself.
Pray for those who never arrived.

The Right
Kimberly Johnson

You have the right to say whatever your heart desires
But lack the right to avoid the consequences
  associated with whatever strings your heart deigns to pull on.
You have the right to remain silent-
But hardly ever do you exercise that type of restraint
Instead you flap your tongue and gums like talking
  is some sort of Olympic sport and you are next in line for the gold medal
You have the right to bare arms
The ability to protect what is yours
But all to often you seem to forget that there's a distinction
  between offended and protective
And many times you do less good and more harm with your arms-
Like there's no body to which you're connected…
Did you forget about us?
The body who makes up your community?
You have the right to pursue that which makes you happy
And some places have even given you the ultimate gift-
I mean, right, to roam free-
Where you are just allowed to be.
You can even stop and take a look see, if that's what you wish.
You have the right to your own identity.
It's a high crime when anyone attempts
  to take this thing that is rightfully yours
And so serious is it taken that-
That when police request it be given,
You have the right to retain that information.
But more often than not,
You give it freely,
Unconscious that a robbery is in progress.
You have the right to believe in whatever deity you choose to see
Or not see
Because you also have the right to not believe in anything.
And yet,
You spend more of your waking hours trying to convince
  the universe that your thought process,
  god or stars are the true, correct and ultimate course
  instead of spending your time in focused worship.
And as I already mentioned-
You've the freedom to discuss whatever you think

is of the utmost importance in your assembly-
Even if what you say is quite offensive to me.
That's the irony of this right given to us
And how hate groups like the KKK were allowed to be birthed-
At least here in the U.S.
You have the right to be free.
NO ONE has the authority to place you in captivity.
There are reasons why this thing called slavery
has been denounced in every country.
Yet, you've allowed yourself to answer to the beck and call constantly…
If only just mentally…
Why do you choose for your mentality to be enslaved in such a way?
You have the right to lodge your complaint
and you have the right to disagree.
You've the right- whether others like it or not-
to protest- even if that means taking a knee.
And when the police act villainously, as they often do-
You have the right to say, however, hoarsely, "I can't breathe."
Because, ultimately, you have the right to be alive.

Ruins

C.Creative

I'm still trying to figure out why you
fell into my life the way you did
It quite literally felt like the sky
crashed down on us
I knew the promises we were making
were tainted
Like our poisoned blood
Dripping and oozing from the saddest eyes
We have had lifetimes of thorns in our hearts
And we were always going to pierce our flesh
without even having touched
I have never known a longing or ache
quite like it
It's an ocean of waves
Pushing me under
While hope is giving me the only strength
I have left just to reach the fucking shore
It's a force so mighty
That brings me to my knees
Shuttering my image
Replicating my mother's pain,
while we pour another drink the same
You see, I fall in love with broken
With no intentions of changing it
Broken to me, is like staring into the eyes
of the devil and seeing a home that still
loves you
That isn't afraid of the burning hell inside you
That is why I found a home in you
Trying to explain us to anyone is pointless
It was a love that formed its own entity
entirely
It was a love that no mortal would understand
It was a love already destined to be in ruins
before I breathed your name

VIRAL OUTBREAK

Red Dust
Kelly Van Nelson

I wore white once, bronze shoulders, blue garter, gold ring,
strolled the aisle with pride, you by my side,
bound by our partnership oath.
Honeymoon wanderlust, credit card bust,
I was me, you were you, we were us,
two decades ago, before red dust.

I was me once, northern girl with the English fair skin,
you were you once, African boy, our souls were akin,
we were us once, no money, but inseparable.
Carved a life on a dime, I learned how to rhyme,
entry ticket into the land of red dust.
Now I free flow, while you FIFO,
but I'm still me, you're still you, we're still us.

When the beat in life changes, it fucks you up,
roll with it, suck it up:
High viz, steel caps, two weeks on,
barbeque, jujitsu, two weeks off,
red dust, no us, two weeks on,
red lipstick, date night, two weeks off,
red dust, two weeks on,
red lipstick, two weeks off,
red dust, red lipstick, red dust, red lipstick,
two weeks on, two weeks off, two weeks on, two weeks off,
I'm still me, you're still you, we're still us, red dust.

You flew out, two weeks on, that was then,
before COVID pandemic claimed our men,
and women and them, the old, vulnerable.
Now our airlines are bust and you're beached in red dust;
I'm alone behind mask to protect
viral particles taking hostage of breath.
Borders closed with me east while you're in the west,
different time, different place, watch sunset – marriage test.

We call and we zoom and facetime,
Whatsapp, RUOK, I ask you.
Ek kan nie nou praat nie, you tell me.
I can't speak at the moment, ok.
Whatsapp, RUOK, Whatsapp, RUOK,

ek kan nie nou praat nie, RUOK?

I'm still me, I'm still here,
you're still you, you're still there,
we're still us, on the east and the west.
Forty weeks, not two weeks, was the on,
permission slip to make a trip home,
red lipstick back on, all dressed up,
barbecue, Jujitsu, two weeks off.

Each day a reborn honeymoon,
skin to skin not on Facetime or Zoom,
but too soon you've to pack, quarantine or the sack,
me and kids on end of the phone, you alone.
ISO / SOS / ISO / SOS / ISO / SOS / RUOK?

We do what we do and we love over Zoom,
I'm still me, I'm still here,
you're still you, you're still there,
we're still us on the east and the west, red dust.
FIFO, ek kan nie nou praat nie,
ISO, ek kan nie nou praat nie,
FIFO / RUOK / ISO / RUOK /
FIFO, ek kan nie nou praat nie.

When dust settles the red tape gets cut,
I'm still me, you're still you, we're still us.
We're red dust / SOS / we're red dust / SOS /
we're red dust, not ok – SOS.

You're On Mute

Fraser Gordon

Voice can't be heard
2020's absurd.
You're on mute

Covid mask wearing
To hide lips whilst swearing
You're on mute

Socially distanced drinking
Our economy's sinking
You're on mute

Family bubbles
Job keeper troubles
You're on mute

Hard fast state borders
Public's disorders
You're on mute

QR code scanning
Disaster flames fanning
You're on mute

Imposed isolation
Confine our nation
You're on mute

Meetings through Zoom
Working in your bedroom
You're on mute

Relatives dying
See people crying
You're on mute

The Phone Call
Skylar J Wynter

We've been expecting a phone call,
delivering a message that's becoming normal.
Not confined to here or there but global.
The second set to the first wave of something viral
that has swept across borders and oceans,
bringing oceans of tears to our borders.
And that phone call came today, caller ID on display.
We knew the words, 'I'm sorry I have bad news',
would put into jeopardy the financial security of our family.
Instead the words, 'I'm sorry, a colleague has passed-away at home',
came down the line in a flat monotone
and we instantly recognised, the words were code for suicide.

We have seen since the onslaught of Covid-19
the globalisation of human suffering.
Humanity reaching out whilst staying in
posting and streaming all manner of things
in an attempt to circumvent alone manifesting.
But the need for sanitation and isolation
has triggered an inclination towards profit rectification
and a new pandemic featuring set after set
of job loss setbacks and backs set back into corners
there is no escape from, is creeping up behind us.
So far, in WA we have not experienced a second wave
of the global pandemic that has tsunamied down on others less fortunate.
So far, we have not felt the extreme hopelessness
of hundreds or thousands of deaths per day clocking up.
We are free to move about our state, shop and socialise
without in your face, cover your face, restrictions, or effort.
But a phone call we thought would be notifying us of a job loss
has left us crushed.
And somewhere out there a family is grieving because
a job loss became a life lost.
A man's name on a FIFO roster
has been permanently crossed off.
Any chance of being rostered back on
or attending his child's first birthday is forever gone.
Any opportunity to tell him, things will be okay,
vanished in an instant today.

This was not the intent, when the company with operations globally
started talking redundancy to cut costs to preserve profits that realistically,
even if halved, would still be profit enough to ensure no person on their
payroll
need be told they are unnecessary.
It was not their intent to leave a child, a family, a wife,
with a human shaped hole in their life.
But they did. And I have to wonder if
They could offer up stability instead
while humanity is experiencing a shift
Not all of us have the scope to survive or deal with
I have to wonder if
the decision makers in these companies know
new facilities are not the only thing they can spread across the globe.
Do they know they could choose to extend anything?
So why not hope?

Instruction Panel

Gerald Kells

kills all known children, should not be
used on germs, comes with its own
delivery method, handle with rubber
gloves, do not get on your skin or eyes,
seek medication if you suffer an allergic
reaction, do not use in front of witnesses
who may survive to tell the UN or where
there may be photographic evidence, do
not mix with forensics, always apply as
directed, packaging is recyclable - available
in aerosol, cream or explosive container,
comes in a variety of colours -

if you are unhappy with any part of this
product a freephone number is provided

Pandemic Mormor (For Torne Madden Zarzana)

Marianne Murphy Zarzana

Dear grandson,
in my dreams, you're growing up too fast.

Last night, in a Swedish dreamscape,
I struggled to pick you up, but—too heavy,
too strong—you squirmed free from my arms,
and darted across your distant lawn, laughing.

Our travel plans to be with you this summer—
COVID-dashed—your mother, your videographer,
now brings you to life on a computer screen.
You reach for a book on the shelf, choosy
at 15 months. When I say the name
of your dog, Gogi, you cross the room,
crouch, and pet the ancient Shih Tzu.

Yesterday, on a Zoom call, your *morfar* and I
watched you toddle around a Swedish campsite.
The sea breeze lifted your golden-red curls,
half a continent and an ocean away.

I'm grateful for the magic of technology,
but more grateful for the moment I held you,
only hours after your birth, Midsommar's dawn,
beside your exhausted, enraptured parents.

Your *mormor* longs for flesh, the blessing
and the necessity of touch.

But do not slow down, sweet Torne.
You're just like your mother
who grew up too fast
though right within our reach.

In Sickness We Are One

Julia Kaylock

The world divides
Clusters contemptuous
Bubbles are nebulous
Conspiracy theories vociferous.

People divide
Freedom withstands
Duty demands
Isolation, we wash our hands.

Time divides
Past freedom mourned
Present overdrawn
Future unborn

Everywhere
In grief, in care,
In dark despair
Humanity is united.

Exiled
Anne Casey

We flew with the wind,
sank our feet deep
　　　　into foreign soil,
　　　　drank thirstily

from the poisoned
spring of these mighty
　　　　nations, worshipped
　　　　at the false altar.

As we look now across
all the tumbled wreckage
　　　　from your displaced
　　　　shore to mine,

might we wonder
how we have come
　　　　to this, to this, to this–
　　　　to this slow folding

-in to this abyss
of our own
　　　　creation: how we had
　　　　failed to mother

Earth, suckled
at the flaccid
　　　　paps of Mammon,
　　　　feasted on the spoiled

flesh of dying
species, fleeced
　　　　by specious
　　　　prophesies–

taken down now
not by those great
　　　　dreaded nuclear war heads
　　　　but by *this*–

this microscopic
Armageddon; still to be human

is to persist
even at this

infernal pass,
we will stir
the will to lean
into the light.

Poleaxed

Anne Casey

We
check // her
temper at ure at reg ular
inter vals, alrea dy knOw ing the
ans wer // our fell ed be aut y loll s
in fever ish d reams // e ach b r e a th a lab our:
her l un gs in flame d // all her art eries slOw ly
c logging // cutt ing of f her legs has not s av ed her:
she is s O t ired no w // e ach palp it at ion of her he art
a suffer an ce: she ach es ever y w here for her l o s t
l im bs, l im ply gr ieving her be love d dead // we check
her temper at ure at reg ul ar in ter vals // alrea dy
kn Ow ing the ans we r: an other two de gr ees & she's
coo ked: cat as trophi c c ell ul ar de c ay // a cute r
esp ira tor y di stre ss cO me s ne xt, ent ire spec
ies annihil at ion // Gaia is blee ding fr
O m h e r e y e s // fr Om in s ide:
f r O m O ur h and s // we 're h e r
k ill er st (r)
a i n

The 'New' Normal
Megan Chapman

How will I know when my 'new' normal has begun?
I doubt there will be fanfare, fireworks and announcements.
There was nothing like that at the end of my 'old' normal.
Well,
there were announcements,
But I didn't recognise
that they were redefining my 'normal',
slowly,
in incremental diminishments.
It felt like I was caught unawares
by the sudden ceasing
of all that made up my 'normal'.

Musing how my 'new' normal might look,
I recall my 'old' normal,
My coffee always ready for me to grab
From his coffee cart
as I passed
on my way to the office.
That welcome nugget of comfort
that set the tone for my day,

Gone.

No chat or names
just a shared passion for good coffee
our morning ritual,

Gone.

Irrevocably ruptured,
Evaporated,
By something smaller than a single coffee ground.

I wonder how he's doing,
And I pine for that coffee.

Christmas Tree Pandemic
Angela Costi

Symptom 1
My little sister would have been three
when she first caught the spread of tingles.
The fever to screech at the sight
of the alien green.

Symptom 2
A seasonal onslaught of corner creepage
stalked by age-defying foliage
in rooms called living, spaces titled reception.
Bairnsdale Hotel of all places,
sipping weak coffee,
reading of fires that focus on trees with souls,
sipping with the ever-present stare
of foreign familiar,
each bauble a *Novel Corona Virus*
determined to cling.

Symptom 3
This year, the tree will continue to run for office
and win
with lights circling out of control,
blinking blazing bodyjamming
absorbing our sleep,
our poetry will not suffice as gift.

Symptom 4
I have been known to gaze adoringly
at the manufactured splendor,
each out-stretched prickle
bejeweled with a colour surprise,
a whimsical fantasy of life without misery.

Symptom 5
Should we pity the tree
grown like cattle, pigs, chicken, sheep,
a tree invested in the almighty grip
of the triangle embrace,
not even Jesus could shake?
Should we pity our lives
using the step ladder,

forever grafted to brittle appendage,
dangling as trinket of lowerarchy,
as heirloom of hierarchy,
as one per cent dictator?
Who gets the gold star?

Illness/State

Claire Language

Spit! I am sick
doctor says sit down girl, sit down.
Ok. I guess I can.
I can do (whatever) you want.
Wash your face girl.
wash it.
Ok. I am okay.
Malleable like chalk
okay girl, okay.
I can leak
all over your perfect floor.
this soluble sultry beast
this puzzle without a piece.
ok girl.
hold it in
hold it in, please.
I can give you, please take a ticket
I can write you a speech
take a break
but I'm not ready?
ok girl, your hearts low,
your legs are okay.
okay girl, ok
spit girl
how many more?

Stay Safe

Devika Brendon

So now it's come - the brewing storm
The invisible worm that flies everywhere
And burrows into every aperture
Our past negligence's have brought to bear.

We should welcome the wearing of masks with others
But remove the distorting glasses from our own eyes.
Let all the untruths and facile lies burn
And those who tell them cease to churn
The giant lottery of truth and compromise
That is now spinning; and will soon be spun.

The Internal External Conscious Mind

Kayin Van Nelson

Once a man who knew so little, time spent milking dull sorrows.
Now, gnashing teeth gnaws on thin skin, chewing neck, mixing blood –
Mind convulses. Grey eyes glossing, creating world rose-tinted.
Thousand sirens symbiotically questioning, answering –
Whining hive pulsing goals of unity. Eat, walk, eat, create.
Viral bluetooth connecting …

Brain rewiring.

Upgraded system hardware deteriorates mobility:
Bones crunch, skin peels, teeth decay, muscles burn. Thoughts explode.
Movement broken, human jealousy fueling comatose rage.
We slither arms around a warm package, preparing shipment.
Life gushes down parched throat, dies in stomach. Gift delivered.
Mind added to database:

Zombification.

Others conspire plans for universal assimilation,
No queen on a high pedestal, only equal shared consciousness.
More than individualism. More than codependency;
Evolution of species. Intelligent Virus sharing knowledge.
A better world: No emotions, no opinions, only basic existence,
Eradication of us –

But who am I? We?

Memories are driftwood camouflaged in murky brown sea. Lost.
Identities are struck from history, nameless silhouettes.
Knowledge becomes empty dirt plain stretching eternally –
Where sheep graze but do not frolic, a herd lost its shepherd.
Blind disciples thrive in comforting community. Together.
Darwinism hits its peak —

–Forward = Direction–

So you walk a thousand miles, see world gone cold devoid of life.
Desolate streets trace dark houses but lamp posts pool unearthly glow –
Against earth untrodden by guilt or love, only footprints seeped
with transcendency. 'Survivors' cherish in stolen hearts
The trappings of long mortality, left behind to find own path.
But, there is still much beauty.

Conscious awe engaged.

Kaleidoscope of images shared by travelling brethren,
Their journeys pixelated slideshows shuttering on clean train –
Passing through vision in momentary flashes, collective ecstasy.
Snow-capped mountains, livid burnt forests, picturesque crystalline caves.
Slumbering towns: Cars painted with green vines, decorating tarmac.
Trees cracking roots through corpses.

Nature outlives death.

Perhaps our end was imminent to reach higher functioning
Separate organisms no longer viable option.
Did God tamper with his own creation? Fixing ancient glitch?
Too many souls in heaven, now only one stranded on Earth.
A walking relic of past unseen. Dead below cranium.
Is this what was meant to be?

Time's but an obstruct.

Heartless body ushers fractured conjoined hearts to Mount Kailash–
Where Ravana, the evil scholar, makes known his bleak presence.
Moving mass of undead flesh stains pleasant desert countryside.
Benevolent cloudless sky collects pleas in Pandora's box –
Never to be opened again. Those who are beyond great blue,
See green and grey and nothing more. No yellow light pollution.
No synergic zombie hell.

Only dreams of home.

Skin to skin, rot spreads like wildfire, Virus stitches separate limbs.
Zombies become zombie. Virus becomes Man. Mountain stands still.
Uncontrolled spasm, body twists unnaturally, spine snaps!
Exosphere stretches to house soma. Joy not mine seeps through veins.
Newborn baby learning ropes, world new present wrapped in duct tape.
I sink into murky ink.

Rise! Rise! Breathe again!

I was malware in Virus binary code – drowned in old tool.
Abandoned atmosphere mutes quietness, dulls sensibility.
Carton of cognition expired, swirling tentacles only

Presence, cushions sleepless spirit. Exit so far above
Red-rimmed ring lustful for romance, can't handle loneliness.
Pity to those infected,

Pity to those who aren't

Consumed. Let the human remnants die, let Virus die with them.
Submicroscopic infectious agent verse opposable thumbs,
Each either side of locked frosty window, looking out looking in.
Fist smashes glass, lets snow billow, blocking window for winter.
Dusty couch contains cordial roommates. Television tuned to
Omnipotent news broadcast.

Ends where it began.

Though now the room is empty. The rain has washed away the snow.
Screen flickers images against peeling paint. Admired by none
But wary traveller, pack grown heavy upon bony shoulder
Who stays night in cramped mossy room, bean cans masking scent
Of buried hatchet. She dreams first the days of walking cancer
When sun feared rising. Then reminisces on past separation.
Finally, wrapped in blankets,

Let's new crescent moon shine pale.
Let's stars shimmer without interference.
And let's planet orbit, godspeed!
Godspeed!

CONSUMED

Way Back When
Kelly Van Nelson

Way back when glass-bottled milk would decorate doorstep
Postie's knock would brighten each day
Bank teller counted coins in the palm of her hand
Ice cream van would serve kids after play

Way back when we drank coffee that came from a jar
Before baristas frothed latte and ground beans
Fish and chips wrapped in newspaper was dinner out
When we managed to budget around meagre means

Way back when lead paint decorated babies cot
Dormant asbestos insulated roof
Miners knew not a thing of black lung disease
In those years before confronting proof

Way back when a typist was sought out for speed
Shorthand a premium skill
When memos didn't come on yellow post-it notes
They were written in ink with a quill

Way back when we realised the world had changed
New jobs beginning to pave way
For careers of the future instead of the past
It wasn't just way back when, it's today

The Oligarchs' Last Supper

Trevor Burndred

After having captured all the trade,
an uneasy truce amongst them was made.
Most of the population has now died.
In spite of 'Freedom' groups – oh how they tried.
The 'End Game' was not that long ago.
The last 12 months has been dog-eat-dog – no fair go.
Thirteen at this table of 'Emperors'.
News Corp in the middle with six oligarchs each side.

This group now controlled the world.
Is this what success looks like?
Outside of these families only service staff are left.
All other life outside of this domain is gone.
These people had the best advice and knew what was coming.
This win at all costs mentality never stopped humming.

Now confined to their 'bunkers' this group are nearing the end.
The larders were stocked for only two years
They can now see that this is all going to end in tears.
Tipping Points were passed and sent the weather systems haywire.
Super Storms, wildfires, droughts, crop failures.
Arctic ice is no more. Methane oozes from the Stepps,
like an effervescent Swchepps.
Manhattan Is drowned. 50 feet under.
Mt Erebus in Antarctica has erupted causing a major meltdown.

They were warned. They knew – hedged their bets.
Human kind only now. All pets have died – no vets.
Vegetation is sparse – virtually a barren landscape.
Empathy not their strongpoints – no regrets.

All coastal cities gone.
All other life bloods have ceased. Such a yawn.
No electrical grids, no water, no food, no comms.
With 60° in the shade – no fear of bombs.
The Atlantic Gulf Stream has stopped.
All of Europe and the British Isles are now in a freeze.
If there were some left they could walk the Channel with ease.
With all their money the Oligarchs could not conquer aging.
They secretly cloned themselves 35 years ago while debate was still raging.
Being still a relatively new science, repercussions were not explored.

A cruel blow to their plans – the final sword.
A clone's fertility only lasts until age 30,
so no more additions to the Family Tree.
No technicians or men of science were spared.
As the machines around them broke they stayed unrepaired.

Because they were going to live forever,
no Last Will & Testaments. Oh, so clever.
From Steve Jobs' deathbed – words so nice.
"Don't educate your children to be rich
Educate them to be happy so that when they grow up they will know the value of things -
Not the price".

These words are engraved on the
Tombstone of Mankind.

Progress
Fraser Gordon

Influencers.
Social mediocrity.
Influenced?

Opinions spinning whilst pinning hopes on the thinning
and dimming of our thoughts which are brimming
with desire to own the latest iPhone.

Click bait. Fake news.
No news but views and reviews on Kanye West's shoes
or who Donald trump sues after blowing a fuse.
I'm bored of their ooze.

Cyberbullying. Cybercrime. Everything's cyber,
the whole worlds online, we're ahead of our time,
and it's our time to shine but the world's in decline
and I pine for the time when everyone was fine.

We're not fine.

The world is a start-up but we're not being smart.
Obsessed with adding the latest gadget to our cart.
And now everything's art?

What happened to patience and hard work?

Instant gratification is the heart of our nation.
Want it now. Need it now. Have it now.
Buy now, pay later, borrow more, see ya later.

Mountains of debt no one will ever climb,
while billionaires become trillionaires.

Well maybe they're fine.
Driving electric cars to work in a coal mine.
The paradox of our time.

It Depends
Mike Mackay

Got Globalised,
Got Connected.
Salary dependent.
Mine went up,
My brother's went down,
He doesn't like this.
I do
How did it happen?
He doesn't know,
Neither do I,
Though far away,
My brother I help when I am able,
His face I see on a screen,
Not across the dinner table.

It's A Small World
Fin Hall

Thinking is difficult, that's why most people judge
Why some people make assumptions
And assumption is the mother of all fuck ups
Where people's dreams are controlled by others
It's such a small world, on repeat
Where the street is not a safe place to be
And today is tomorrow's history
A history that today we don't learn from
We don't concern ourselves overmuch over
Where children die of hunger
And their father dies of the want of respect
Because the white man, the far-right man,
Thinks the left man, the bereft man
Is a lesser man.
It's a small world on repeat
And corporations pay millions to other corporations
But little to the taxman.
And pay no attention to those who
cannot afford to pay into their businesses
The situation then becomes a fight between wrong and right
Right and left, left behind and go ahead
Living, dying, dead
It's a small world on repeat
When you look at Schrodinger's coffin, do you wonder
If inside and outside are both the same
Can you play and not play the game?
But, and it's a big but,
When we care for all, does it really mean all
Should we care for those that hate
Those that want to rule and ruin?
Those that don't care?
It's a small world on repeat.
The enemy doesn't arrive by boat
He arrives by limousine
The enemy isn't always within
Sometimes they are without
Without a moral guide,
And convenient amnesia.
With reference to the 'relentless war',

you appear to have thrown the pin at the enemy,
but left the grenade in your trench.
It's a small world on repeat
When you have no home, and steal milk
You end up in jail
When you are a royal pervert
You get a medal
When you are a Tory manager
A paedophile to boot
You get a slap on the wrist
they can't be trusted
It's just one lie after another
even when they're
caught out they'll try and
blame someone else.
It's a small world on repeat
It's a small world, but wide.

The Clock Is Ticking

Trevor Burndred

Fools ponder their mortality
Whilst waiting at the end of a rope.
The Ferryman is already half way across.
What am I leaving my grandchildren?
Money is not digestible.
Time to wake up.
The politicians are just, well, politicking.
The earth is still heating
The blame game is on.
No votes in doing the right thing,
Economics will again have its way.
Maybe, just maybe,
Economics ***WILL*** have the sway.
A revolution is now underway.
The New Money is not going to fossils.
Renewable is the new war cry –
More jobs, greater returns.
Follow the money.
Now the race is on.

Plastic

Markey Mark Symmonds

Oceans blue and green, whales floating, swimming in seas of rubbish, cess-pools of fools discarded plastic wrappers and throwaway nappies designed to keep us humans happy. Scientific invention the plastic revolution part of Darwin's evolution. No solution to plastic pollution new resolution.

Fish dying while MP's lying, hiding behind mediocre gestures while the planet festers in the name of progress. We have regressed leaving our waste all over rivers seas and space. We need to pick up the pace, straws and bags are the political grace of the carbon-neutral politicians two-faced. Flying to conferences in jet aircraft burning fuel at a mighty pace to meet leaders face to face as the world moves at a deathly pace.

Yesteryear, some hold dear, our recycling credentials were clear. while we were burning fossil fuels milk bottles were being reused, delivered on electric carts during early morning starts and the rag and bone man with his horse and cart, no one complained about methane from the horse's fart.

Was Darwin right about adaption of the species survival of the fittest? interpreted by government as survival of the richest. Evolution is killing us, the convenience and speed we want it all plastic was that delivery tool. Now we have exploration into space, as our planet lays to waste, when its dead the rich will flee to the moon instead, dodging the junk, they have dumped above our heads. Leaving the poor to live with the mess that's left, reduced to seas of plastic and shores of decaying gannets, sucking dry the last air on this dying planet.

Sharecropper

Gerald Kells

I am not a slave,
I am a sharecropper,
my produce is the world's,
my coffee, my sugar,
my labour under the beating sun
my fingers are grooved with dirt,
the rows of pink carnations which I cannot eat -
in return I'm given poverty, debt, hunger,
a wage for this production
over which I have no control -

I am not a slave,
I am a sharecropper,
I share in the drugs I cannot afford,
the disasters I cannot escape
and the opportunities taken from me,
I share in death but I get more of it and earlier
and coffins are so expensive -

but I am not a slave,
I am a sharecropper,
I am proud of my freedom
even when it is illusory,
even when I see you on the other side of the road
sneering over your prescription glasses,
muttering: what's your problem now, sharecropper,
didn't we make you free?

Reflections
Fraser Gordon

Isolation is a justification
for the rumination of our generations' devastation

The speed of our greed forced us to concede
that our need to succeed would never recede

Churning, yearning, learning, always earning
but never concerning because the worlds' turning

Until it stops.

The World Is On Repeat
Susan Wakefield

And then he uttered,
"I wasn't defeated, but betrayed in an age where lethal oligarchs strayed
Perverts with nice hair
Told me to beware, 'case I disobeyed..."

The world is on repeat

In a territory new that dictates rule—who knew?
The Progression disease has won
Itself, a viral shedding delivers a new message, soft and plum
Of a contagion disease wedding: the new normal is not normal
Just look what we've become—plastic plants, dichotomous fun?
Faulkner Dear Faulkner, I fear the New World Order
Mondialization
Where violence after violence governs disorder of the day
Stuck in a vortex of turning, we say,
But: we're "moving forward," aren't we?
Progression rules, moving four to the ward, ball and chain,
To where, no one knows—around and around again
A liquidating fantasy reigns in secret global destinies
Entities where rich apex eaters blow dollars out their nose, money hoes
(The new elitists of the night)
Their tongues, sideward slung, eat the underdogs in fright
Shut out your neighbour! Lock up your kids!
Under a half yellow sun we've fallen to bits

The world is on repeat

The record player is stuck, this dynasty of violence passed on—
We've run amok in a sick new language of Apple insignia
This prison camp of playthings
The fallen fruit we eat up
How we suffer pleasantly when the bell tolls
(irritable bowel syndrome, dining on caviar, first world problems, nobody knows)
Detachment from reality's sword, there's nothing we cannot afford (except sanity)

The world is on repeat

Watch us crumble, return to prehistoric dust—as we must—

To learn the lesson of fools
My Orwellian gumboots are brimstone full
My desiccation sucked dry of Socratic discussion
In regimented chaos we float away from the question
Into a politically correct play of lies
Why why why why why
Distracted by emojis, windswept on twitter feeds
Facebook flat face to fill empty identity needs
Deprived of intellectual vitality
Washed down in dryadust prose
Desex my state, tell me I know nothing now—
I am but an archaic Pettifogger
My fossilised thoughts may as well flap wild on Bengali tongue
Loose of lips, drizabone I've become (in my activism of minus one)
I sit, obsolete behind progression's wide berth
Repeat Repeat Repeat! Globalisation at my feet!
It's getting worse;
Burning in my seat I see this in the dearth of things
Slavery is freedom, clean and neat
We cannot unsubscribe from Hell now
Listen to the chyron; hear its silent cry across the room tell more lies
Erase you as you suckle at its breast—turn dry
I xertz my truth into silence like a fine grained silica-rich crystalline meth
I am nothing more than diatomaceous earth,
Hacked and strangled to death in the most silent of ways
I am the jolt of every slow, quiet wringing out of my days
By the one that never lays a hand on my skin, only suffocates the voice with-
in
I pray, for we have become the sum of all and nothing
In a New World Order for One; the cupboard is bare, over there
Dissolving dialectical as the set of all rational numbers (did somebody say
rational?)
One by one, slides off the page
Into a living grave of Worldization

The world is on repeat

In my non-prescient stage, memorandum to one
Under a quiet and vague revolt too deep to draw upon
I am nothing but the lowly sediment sucked through the straw

Of a thousand years lost or more, shackled by progress in our becoming—
We wear masks now, just to be more 'comfortable'
Did it work? Is anyone asking?
Alive and dead—free and constrained
Rotting in a revolting petrie dish of sin, our living grave
Dare ye not maketh a din on this groupie progression bus
We've worked hard enough to lose the essence of Us

The world is on repeat

Enough!
Give me the ordinary
Ameliorate us from pejoration.

Junkies In The Underpass: Below St Philips Causeway, Bristol
Caroline Burrows

I cycle quickly past,
The junkies in the underpass.
Their dealer stands dead centre,
A white man dressed in black,
Astride a bike, with no lights.
This underworld, his stage.

Evenin', brays this king,
Of short sharp pricks,
As I ride wide of him,
Peddling his shit,
To two locals laid low,
Between the broken glass and grit.

His shout carries a glint,
Like the water in the bottle,
And the tarnished metal spoon,
I spy left, at pedal level.
A scene waning,
Like the moon.

Yellow light reveals them huddled,
Beneath the underpass' mosaics,
Which depict a long history,
Of most of Bristol's trades.
This current exchange excluded,
And the sugar, and the slaves.

Graffiti scrawls across the pictures.
Letters and words all strung out.
Not street art,
Not a Banksy.
Just a public place defaced.
It's an update, representing,
This exact time and space.

Zoommobile
Jeff Cottrill

Hey baby. Wanna see the world with me?
Wanna reach out and touch each other's souls
Across a bright and infinite landscape?
Or wanna leave your bedroom after midnight
For crêpes and coffee on the Champs-Élysées,
All in an instant?

Baby. Just hop inside my ZoomMobile.
My ZoomMobile is gonna take you high
And land you safe and sound wherever you say.
My ZoomMobile is gonna fly you away
To the four corners of the blessed earth
Before you even rise up from your bed.
My ZoomMobile will bring us both together
Like no planes, trains or even automobiles
Could ever dream of.

A ride on ZoomMobile don't cost me nothin'.
The dealership was overstocked that day
And gave the ZoomMobile away for free.
My ZoomMobile don't take no gasoline.
My ZoomMobile runs on electric power.
I plug the mother in, so I can come
And plug you in, baby.

The ride in ZoomMobile is always smooth.
No bumps, no swerves, and no collision risk.
We can get smashed on pills and cheap champagne;
The cops will never pull us over, babe,
And every journey's safe as a baby's womb.
And what a trip it is, my wandering mate.
We'll go and dive into a pool of art
And culture, full of shallow ends and deep,
From every civilization 'round the globe.
We'll crash the private bedrooms and the dens
Of folks you'd otherwise never get to meet.
Hear poetry in London and New York,
Talk politics in Belgium and Brazil,
Go see Australian seminars – or just
Kick back with pints of beer and garlic bread

With everyone at once.

So baby, let us go then, you and I,
And ride this magic carpet through the sky,
And see the world without no airline fare.
Get out of my dreams and into ZoomMobile.
(Just don't forget to unmute.)

Looking Down On Humanity
Julia Kaylock

Humans, the highest rung on creation's ladder
lurching from one bad decision to another in fast succession,
hungry for wealth, everlasting life, and more booze
to slake an unimaginable thirst
to forget ...
racing to the ever-shifting finish line
without ever realising the rules
keep
changing
keeping us on our well-shod toes
important things to do, coffee fuelled hedonists
not seeing
not listening

no time for reflection, thoughts about cause and effect,
no self-respect for the skin we're in
or what's underneath
moving through windows of opportunity into vaults of obscurity,
putting on the cloak of invisibility, changing face, masks in place
heading in the wrong direction
far away from anything that resembles
loving or affection
for fellow humans, or other creatures,
or the planet.

David Attenborough should do a documentary on humans.
Then again, he would probably just be happy if we all disappeared

Oh the irony.

Change

Markey Mark Symmonds

Change not to the other default position that just leads to more division and government derision. Shifting the chairs is just the same outcome but from a different position.

When MPs vote against children's nutrition but still take their rise reflecting their status and position then you have to conclude that this is not a sincere position but merely to rock the boat of the opposition.

When climate change is an urgent message yet the reality is massaged. When the speed of change is painfully slow and the government don't want us to know that they have the power to and the know how to create a revolution with sustainable solutions yet eco systems die because of corporate ties when they move the soil to new locations hoping to populate the new destination so that trains flow fast into northern stations.

No, it's not just a case of putting a mask on your face and a cross in the box every four years the same vox pops that never stop. Old ideas recycled and watered down no big picture or blue sky thinking while the ice caps are melting and landfill is stinking. Russian oligarchs more important in their thinking .

With a swoop of the pen they could eradicate fuel poverty yet still they play wait and see as the old get mugged by elected thugs and we follow like slugs. The radicals are rising it's hardly surprising when politicians are hiding under immigration legislation that forgets people are humans and over consuming while those in the camps are left for years amongst squalor and tears.

Change has to come soon a radical monsoon that soaks the political elite from their heads to their feet and a new dawn is spawned and the planet reborn. I'm not talking traditional uprising from controversial hypocrites no better than the other shits disorganised and falling to bits no what we need is a new generation fixing their nation not trying to destroy other dictations. Lead by example for all not just your wealthy sample that secretes on the underclass that you keep short of brass thirty-two a class. Change for us all to embrace not just for money but to save the human race.

Sell Me Your Diamond

Gerald Kells

sell me your diamond
now that you're poor,
what would you need
a diamond for?

I know it is sparkly
and keen as can be
but it's no use to you,
it's much better with me

so sell me your diamond,
here's what I'll pay:
a room full of strangers
with nothing to say

of course it's your diamond
but when it is not
you'll forget that you owned it
and it was worth such a lot

Lessons Unlearned
Trevor Burndred

Have you "Masters" not remembered 1789?
We are fast approaching another deadline.
And all you bystanders are complicit.
For those who do not learn from history will repeat it.
"Let them eat cake all seasons".
Do you fail to see the reasons?

All over the world the cry is going out –
"Alms for the poor", there is no doubt
Compassion has left those that rule.
'Can we not share a ride on your mule?'

Some others ***have*** seen the light.

The very word 'Socialism'
Frightens all those who follow 'Neo-Liberalism'.
Their history books read it as 'Communism'
Something, we are told, that was fought over to oppress.
The money made in the war efforts does not impress.
'Wall Street' does not fear war – they can make a buck.
To the less fortunate it is not bad luck.

The world's purse has enough to share
But those who control the strings do not care.
When some have nothing left to lose, they will pick up their pitch forks again
To get back some of that ill-gotten gain.

A Subjective Invective

Michael Collins

He rides around at his leisure
in a chauffeur-driven limousine:
been to places around the world
you and I have never seen;
flies his own private jet...
busy living The Dream!

Gives no thought for tomorrow-
his dirty hands soon washed clean.

It is the same old story:
the rich keep getting more...
whilst those without the means
continue to stay poor.
Politicians in his pocket!
High-flyers bow and kneel.
What the rest of us may own...
this man will try to steal.
'Life' is life inside the frame
of his next killer deal:
there is no great concern
for any future 'common-weal'.
In the race to the bottom
there is no 'level playing field':
'absolute power' corrupting...
Exploitation revealed!
The light in his eyes
shines green for greed:
I watched him smile in disdain
at portraits of need.
There is nothing he would not do
in order to succeed:
a function of his Neo-liberal
'one-percent-owns-everything'... creed.
Resources appropriated
by the very few!
An entire planet ravaged...
Atonement overdue!

I Live Alone

Geoffrey Aitken

we number
billions
an impending
catastrophe
a mass of uniquenesses
bumped
blended
forged
and strangled
into
a global currency
individually impotent
but unafraid
to randomly
express

in
a selfie

A Global State Of Mind

Franchesa Kirkpatrick

Look at the conveniences we have that
Our great grandparents did not have.
Global.
The time before Wal-Mart
The five and dimes were full of locally made products.
Not Global.
Most places did not have a choice of brands or
Who made what they needed.
Not Global.
Now, the food on our table, the clothes on our backs,
laptops, phones, computers are all made elsewhere.
Global.
The list is endless:
Global clubs, meetings, churches, music,
Faces from distant lands.
Car parts, machine parts, clothes all globally made
Under cheap labour in crowded places around the world.
Trillions of paper dollars being made by millionaires and billionaires
While people cry out globally for relief.
Humans living in a global situation under stress.
Only one solution I can find:
Peace on Earth must be a Global State of Mind.

Rites

Miles Hitchcock

The rite of passage in modern capitalist society
is to copy an image of another
and then have your image copied
by others.

The ego's job
to make us feel good about ourselves
is relentlessly exploited
by the market.

Products bring self-identification
so marketing is psychoanalysis
and media medication.

We don't learn anything anymore.
We are in trance.
Learning goes slower than the information cycle.
Consciousness is being exploited,
minds have been shackled
to larger purposes.
Humans are becoming like algorithms
in a hive mind, moving parts in a eusocial organism,
nodes in an information exchange,
but we have only one wavelength
and the total data does not download.

The Country In Me
Toni Wass

Growing up "Out West" is like a whole different lifestyle,
Where "worldly" city people came to stay—for just a while.
Where laidback locals moved to a slower clock every day,
Life wasn't so stressful when lived the quiet country way.

A progressive 20th Century bought forth inevitable changes,
Iron horses replaced the four-legged kind in various stages.
Road transports took over when steaming river boats retired,
Dust-choked tracks now sealed—and of course city-inspired.

Country people proved to be a resilient breed over the years,
Money worries, droughts, floods—"No time for useless tears!
Come on Mate! —Pick yourself up and fix what you still own."
Resilient backbones stand straight together in every last town.

Into the 21st Century, country towns aren't always the same,
Cafes, B&Bs and 4WD's with aircon are a whole new game.
Though, some townships are slower to embrace "mod cons,"
When it comes to their own patch of dirt—their spirit is strong.

I observe now, upon leaving my hometown so many years ago,
Country folk no longer think badly of those city "So and So's!"
What with broadband and mobile coverage in remote places,
Forced isolations no longer worry locals in wide-open spaces.

Now it seems there are country gourmet cooks everywhere,
Pecans, olives and prize wines help create a distinctive flair.
Not-to-mention, a new breed of Aussie country-raised stars,
Never could our pioneers ever imagine we would roam so far.

"You can take the girl out of the country" - or so the saying goes
But the country stays in my blood - as my heart already knows.
Now as I travel along these congested highways and city streets,
My heritage of being raised as a country girl runs ever so deep.

Faded Glory

Imogen Arate

He headed the Heartbreakers
And died from a heartbreak:
Self induced with substances
Introduced to ward away the pain,
Of songs created from poignant days
Now hocking something insignificant
In 30 seconds of fame.

"Sympathy for the Devil"
Now sells a luxury vehicle
To particular men of wealth and taste
For irony is found in irony lost
When the skimmed surface is valued
And the depth below tossed

Hippies who rocked out for Jimi
Traded tied-dyed for suit and tie
Free love transforms into free hate
For Jimi's kin and kind

Exoticized misunderstood religions
Of others once used to escape
The oppression of elders
In countercultures glorified
Now commercialized in bottled chai
And franchised yoga chains

Sitars strains underlay appropriated refrains
Though appreciation for the culture and people fades
Used and discarded without lasting reparations
Like Afghan poppy fields for many decades since

Though concerts galore raised money for the poor
Starving eyes still implored
For deeper connections and structural changes
Historical relations never explored

Sanguine Imbecility

Geoffrey Aitken

disappointed
again
by morning
headlines
still unable to confirm
our dire
global circumstance
or the hint
of a plan
to steer us clear
but
the status quo
reinforces
with authorized denial
as
worst dreams
expose
polit speak enthusiasm
for business as usual
and
the roguish

'don't you think we know that'

Flood
Des Mannay

River of tears
salty wet
from giving birth
womb of winds
storm of floods
Texas, Louisiana -
death floats in streets

Buffoon flies in
for TV lens
photo opportunity.
Politicians only
talk in numbers,
$7.5 million -
auction begins

South East Asia
levee breaks -
displacement figure
outbids cash of
American leaders.
Numbers crunch
like bullets fired
from a machine gun.

Elsewhere in the
land of the free
corn crops rot as
vast underground lakes,
aquifers, are bled dry;
just caverns now.

Without water
we cannot survive:
with flood water
we cannot survive.
Forget the oil wars -
the next 'great' war
will be for water.

MOTHER NATURE

Crane

Kelly Van Nelson

Crane
Soaring above the rooftops
Neck overextended
Majestic wings spread
Metal frame light as a feather
Elegantly manoeuvring heavy load
Morphing the skyline each day
Before migrating to the next site
To construct new nests

…mother nature meets man's machine

Once Upon A Time There Was A Woman

Maroulla Radisavic

A beautiful woman…
She had many children.
She loved them, she fed them
and nourished them, with her love
and her wisdom.
She showered them with lemon blooms
But the children didn't care.
Once upon a time there was a beautiful woman
Her name was Mother
and she loved her countless millions children
One day she became sick
She sent desperate messages
"I'm leaving…Love me…
Where can I leave my children
Without lemon blooms?"
But the children didn't care
Once upon a time there was a beautiful mother
Her children were called "Humans"
Her name was "Mother Earth"
But the children didn't care…

Achill Sound
Hiram Larew

When the roads curve like sound
        and dip as if lifting to bow
Whenever all thoughts round or cluster
        or when hearts call down
                is Ireland

And as rich when poor was
        or as wise as bare heads in snow seemed
        and as twigs so frail broke into song
        and as true as any blight or potato could be
                was Ireland

So when sand laps the senses
        or salt drips the edges as dreams
Whenever hope streams through such heavens
        and moss comes home
        or hearts beam down
                is Ireland.

A Warning

Margaret Frodsham

Will we read history in the years to come?
Or will the earth be planet on fire?
Will it have no regard for our race or our creed,
but consume us all in its pyre?

Will there be language to grow and to change
so we add some new words every year?
Or will all the hot gases so heat up the globe
that it sweats and it shakes with the fear?

Will newspaper stories still amplify glories?
Or won't there be paper for writing?
So who will report on the wars that we fought-
and the children who died without fighting?

Will poets still muse (and often confuse)
on the sweetness of flowers and trees?
Will they pen a soft lyric to a meter in pyrrhic
when the earth is engulfed by the seas?

Will language just die from the smoke in the sky
and the boom and the crash and the smashes?
Or will Phoenix arise like a bird in disguise-
and save just a spark- from the ashes?

Global Fears Last For Years

Franchesa Kirkpatrick

Global fears last for years
Mother Earth sheds tears
Flooding around the globe

Global fears last for years
Mother Earth cheers
Healing pollution with time

Global fears last for years
Mother Earth is pleased
Seasons bring bounty for the people

Global fears last for years
Mother Earth has to sleep
People start to weep

Global fears last for years
Mother Earth hears
We stand together even when far apart

Global years overcome fears
Mother Earth sings
Balance is restored

Custodians

Glenda Traub

(Dedicated To The Spirit Of All Nations)

Wild flaming
modelled by earth
your eyes speak aeons
of ancient wisdom passed
come to fill the cup of future
full to brimming.

Come to rescue from ourselves separation
from domination
raping and gaping echoing emptiness of land.

Bringing careful hands to gently wipe
our dear earth mother's face
clear of pain
devastation and disgrace.

Custodians
sanctify us with the cross in four directions.
Circle your blessings with a jewel
the desire to unite
to heal
and together we will awaken our oneness.

Starfish

Dane Ince

What is the number of skies
How many moons orbit around us
I am lost like a bag of slices
Bleeding double edged razor blades
This earth is my only earth
And I love her like school boy crush
When she turns and walks away
Dropping my crumpled love note on the ground
Unread
Seduced addiction fills her with corporations' mighty dick
And sleek sophistication too smart for our own good
Gobbles globalization steals everything
And everything and love from this poor boy
With no appreciation for holy scared joy
With no appreciation for what might be
Some distant child's distant distant smile for tomorrow
Face red cool by tears selfish poison
Brazen watching sway of hips ocean hips
Watching as she walks away
Knowing she is dying
Watching
Trashy filled and sick
Under summer cotton dress sways
Watching my lovely love earth slipping walking away
Eternal yearning
Floating plastic mercury in her fish
We come to this
This heartbreak
This bargained bought away from me and us love
She will not look me in the face
She cannot through pollution wink
Wink back she loves me too
The hearts of wage slaves will be broken for a lark
Beaten and defeated
Accepting the giving up
All there is for doing
So when you win
The all there is and waste it
The rest of us ready eat heartily the globalized lie

That Ophelia died by accident
When in fact you murdered her
My earth
My Ophelia
By poisoning killed
Her soul
Her mind
Her sea soil and sky
Withdrawing usuary pimp when finished and laughing
Left me standing and the rest of all
With broken pieces
Of hearts and minds
In our famished hands
Severed starfish join together
Will be coming for you in the end

Where Have All The Lizards Gone?
Margaret Frodsham

In the 1950s my mother battled with millions of marauding flies that
were hell bent on consuming her colandered cabbage.
Ignoring the flies, I watched the engineering ability of ants,
the colour and variety of beetles,
and the beauty of butterflies flitting from plant to plant.
There were hundreds of cheeky small lizards
who seemed to be everywhere and nowhere all at once.
But where oh where are they now?

I rarely see a fly. Maybe a few in the kitchen.
I have searched the garden, but rarely do I see a beetle.
There are white moths aplenty,
but for years, I have not seen a butterfly.
And the lizards? They are so rare
that I want to record the time and date I actually saw them.

Maybe, just maybe, the lack of insects means
that the lizards are starving,
and they carelessly venture too close to the cats.
The cats eat the lizards and the cycle begins all over again.
Soon the cats will be asking: 'Where have all the lizards gone?'

Indigo

Dr. Deidra Suwanee Dees

indigo,

magenta, vanilla

tasting sky

approaching

Breath And Being

Gerard Traub

Upon the march of millenniums
our empires forever rising to fall
traversing paths to timeless oceans
we are breath and being all.

Braved into wondrous light
between tides and boundless skies
into the eyes of humanity
I hear your silent cries.

Lost amidst the shadows cast
such worlds of endless ways
to again remember that we are soul
before the cradle and beyond our graves.

Whether in shallow waters or deep
life led by greater designs
from this blood until our return
neither of earth or flesh confined.

We are breath and being all.

Crossings

Daragh Byrne

1.
The taxi driver, Balkan, tawny, eulogises
The Adriatic. We compare notes, tell our tales
Of trips across the globe, never quite
Knowing where home is, though our beds are here
Our work, our mates — the fabric of our lives
Is wove from antipodes, with thick strands
Of long left lands; heart threads through the twill.
We are well made. Tense cloth that seldom tears.

Three hours before departure; plenty of time
To stretch my mind back through ten years or more —
A sudden reverence for my strong will,
My stubbornness to not make permanent
Any of my returns. Stood like a climber
At the base, testing a taut rope; confident
I will ascend, enjoy the view, be strong
Enough to make it down again.
                                        Whatever
In my nature makes it so, I've long since
Given up the need to know. Distance and
The desert had their way, and I have healed
Enough to feel at peace; to come back to
The land, the stone, the ancestors I'm from.

2.
Squaring up again, ten thousand miles
Takes aim, lands belly blows on my
Circadian
            and down I go.
                                A holy state
the ancients could not know.

What is this strange land that I know so well?
These strangers who I love?
These memories, alive, where once I dwelled?
Years echo in the faces of my dear ones —
In every pair of eyes, the stony deep
Glint of history, given up to wandering gods;
Blood ties boiled to fuel my flight.

There is a sameness to the changed, a shimmering
Layer of temporal instability dusting those
That rise from dust. The faces of the dead
Resound in sons and daughters. I find comfort
In genetics spitting in death's maw;
In the easy way the locals say hello.

3.
The same old friends, same table at the pub
A club of happy phantoms haunting still.
We have been meeting here for twenty years:
Our footprints shone the flagstones on the floor.
Nobody asks me now if I'll move back —
Well-worn routines are how we have the craic.

Sobriety dissolves, a blaze of gin
We circle serious, fuck levity, we're in —
Dissecting arguments we've overdone
By decades, thrusting with a tough familiarity.
Now I am home, remembering why I left,
And why I must keep coming back till death.

4.
I hear the shadow bark of dogs long dead.
I know this house is simply bricks coated
In coarse pebbles, ghosts beneath the floor —
That I am, like my mother, made of cells,
All counting down to apoptosis.

The house breathes out a warning, heavy air
Reminding me like an insistent pup
To turn and leave is risking everything.

5.
I cross again, the cold unnourished light
Of midnight airports shivering my thoughts.
I concentrate, too drained to be distraught,
Helping a woman with a pram down steps
To Abu Dhabi tarmac, jet fuel in my nose,
Holding her sleeping child in blackened heat.
A family's love transported round the earth

With single minded honesty will reach
The farthest land. Love now goes further than
It ever did, but they still weave it from
The same old stuff.
It finds a way to stretch.

Resuscitation

Glenda Traub

Willpower
maelstrom of achievements
what lie would endeavour thus?
Howsoever the red dust of earth's time
wilt the flower of thy being.

Rancour than the jungle's bedfloor
deeper than the pungent odour
of life's narcotic neanderthal
will be the thought of tomorrow
unless
unless we stop it now
stop it in its tracks
hail the necessity of time!

Heroes are gone
lovers are dead
curses are waiting
lurking in the shadows of the darkest minds.
Bring humanity into lighthood
shock them into truth
hurl their misery against the back door
and kick it out!
Should we say further?
Is it clear?
Hyphenated longing
judgement pursuing.

Oneness
elevated to the highest of being
like a dog on the heels
running hastily out of sight.
What's wrong with couth?
Who cut it out of the livelihood of kings?

Justice
trickling down the drain
into the darkness of the night.
Who's scoring now?
I am not!
I've been wronged a thousand times

and righted another thousand
Why not stop counting
stop revenging
stop flicking the knife
coiling the curd
pulling the trigger
hurling the stone
fighting the fight?

Laugh at it we say
give it a grin
let it go into a curving corner of a smile
and in a sparkle of an eye
let it sag like a spent oak.

Coconut

Riya Rajesh

coconut is carried across the air
drips meeting my eyebrows
holding my hair
a weighty waterfall of black
my mother wading through
battling
playground knots
childhood tangles
and her own stories
melbourne's winter keeps windows shut
blankets piled
ugly coats out
i remember sitting cross-legged in early migration
the orange glow of portable heaters
how
they were a danger to nearly-dry-clothes
and six-year-olds
i remember this sacrament
from before i knew it would be
my mother and i
silence, daydreams
blankets
missing and missing different things
getting used to living, difference

each quietly content
brushing connection behind chore,
i hope

Gaia's Lament

Lindy Jelliman

O' Gluttinous Humans!

You are my pandemic.
You crawl all over me, your Earth Mother,
Stifling me with your waste and toxins,
Labouring my every breath.

I bloomed, not only for you, but through my own celestial destiny:

To glow in effervescence, to nurture, to nourish.
To thrive in efflorescence; to flower, to flourish.

From this energy divine
I co-created and birthed abundance;
With un-fettered imagination,
Sculpting beauty at every turn:

Vast and pristine oceans, plumped by creatures
Of such intricate and whimsical design;

Giggling streams, dipped & dappled with life,
Casting ethereal sparkle-rays in the morning sun;

Expansive water torrents, homed by prehistoric life,
Cutting through rock and flora in rapid, falling grandeur;

Mirrored lakes and diamond-splintered fjords,
So lovingly co-forged in glass-blown splendour;

Geological giants, those grandiose and proud pinnacles,
Crowning our landscapes: so intricately clothed in canopied vines and moss;

The open plains, carved with smooth and loving embrace;
Dotingly adorned with creatures of such divine grace and comedy.

All of this was destined to:

Glow in effervescence, to nurture, to nourish.
To thrive in efflorescence; to flower, to flourish.

I co-created and birthed you, my earth children;
Nature's own guardians, to embrace,
Celebrate and NURTURE this abundance!

How then, have you so blindly lost your way?
How is it so that you smother me and my co-creations
In in such poisonous slurry,
Toxically stripping me away?

I have embraced, nursed, nurtured and loved you.
Here I am now as Gaia, your Earth Mother (at her wit's end), imploring you to stop!
Have you not heard my tantrums and seen my tears?
Have you not felt the earth burning hot from my rage
And witnessed the floods of my remorse?

I remind you now:
You are here on my terms (not I on yours);
We are meant to live in harmony together:

To glow in effervescence, to nurture, to nourish.
To thrive in efflorescence; to flower, to flourish.

I ask you, my earth children: "Must you have so much?
Can you not rather live simply and graciously,
Gratefully enjoying what is, instead of seeking more?
For beauty and abundance abounds and it is enough."

Let me tell you this: "by seeking more, you will have less."

RISE! Yes, now!
Bend down, place your hand on the ground;
Touch and caress my soiled and tear-stained face.

REMEMBER! Yes, now!
Do not take me for granted.
Never forget our mutual and abiding love.

PLEDGE! Yes, now!
Pledge to care for me in my advancing years.
I am tired. I need your help.
I just need you to do one small thing for me each day:

Consume less. Grow more. Use less.
Recycle more. Unplug. Drive less.
Turn off a light. Turn off taps.

Plant a tree.
Love me.

Let us now heal our bond, my earth babies.
Let me once again take you to my bosom,
Gently rocking you and singing you to sleep,
With fireflies in your periphery;
The fragrances of jasmine, rose and wisteria
Engulfing your slurred and peace-filled slumber.

For together, it is our divine destiny to:

Glow in effervescence, to nurture, to nourish.
Thrive in efflorescence; to flower, to flourish.

Auto Correction
Devika Brendon

The many-coloured dream coat
does not fit well, or sit well with me:
The numberless calamities of life
Have frayed the fabric thin.
The materials in which I wrapped myself have shredded
with the passing of those I have loved,
and trust, and those I have lost.

Yet life itself goes on, under wraps,
Stubbornly butting its head against us
Like a plant in the frozen ground
Like a newborn small animal
Making its arrogant demands for attention and solace
Am I pregnant with life, full of expectation?
Do I swell with pride
at what I feel inside?

Its fierce small presence and determination comfort me
All the self-help groups tell us to
look within for the answers
And I feel it, determined not to
allow me to subside
and sink under the strong tide.

I hold onto the idea of it,
that very young thing,
my will to live,
shaping me into a whole human being
under the fragile protection of skin.

This Is My Axis

Kelly Van Nelson

I didn't
spin out of control
as a result of your behaviour
but because Mother Earth told me
I was never meant to be
controlled by
anyone

FOUND IN SPACE

Explosive Calamity

Kelly Van Nelson

Four and a half billion years before our two planets aligned
love was cruel, blind, rarely kind,
then lust became my new fossil fuel
boosting solar system energy for a short while,
gravity forcing sublime rhyme,
a nebula blocking out reality
dust and gas fusing us in explosive calamity,
never contemplating we might need revision,
blinded by illusion encrusted in tunnel vision
not seeing the future eclipse of a lifetime together
when I passed you, you passed me, no more we.

Suddenly we were no longer one earth
where we once rose in synchronisation
in correlation with flirtation,
instead we split apart and you became my displaced moon
transforming into the singular solar night light
that fought against my sunset plight
as we circled around each other
in a relationship consuming the galaxy
until that asteroid hit
and I was the only person who didn't see the speed
of the collision hurtling towards me –
no more us, no more they, no more we.

The united journey we once embarked upon
has spun undone and become new sun
rising in a new dawn so slow I know
it's time to catch my breath and decompress,
caught up was I in starry undress,
until nothing could prevent the digress
into extinction of a pair of dinosaur carcass
who were never able to commit with conviction
to a home always destined for eviction
as all we ever could be was a temporary addiction
craving you, ravishing me, consuming we.

We now coexist in a galaxy as separate stars
where women are from Venus and men are from Mars
opposites who met through lust and luck

before grinding to a halt from the mind fuck
of spinning twenty-two Jurassic era hours every day,
cramming in a lifetime of work, rest and play,
morphing into an endless, mindless partnership
where you tried to inhabit my mothership
and I wasn't ready to give in to psychological warfare
knowing we were built on thin air of a wing and a prayer
and I was right to cut loose the disrepair
of lonely heart, needing new start, after we part.

Genesis

Maroulla Radisavic

Witness raw nature
sounds and accents merging
Genesis reborn

Battlescars
Heather Barker Vermeer

"It is not the mountain we conquer, but ourselves."

– Sir Edmund Percival Hillary

The old and tired and lifeless grind was light on joy and folks being kind.
Hunched over phones, they thumbed their moans, in filtered, jilted, jealous tones.
Whose desperate dream, internal scream, and outward grin let nothing in.

Then fear it fell; from north, within. It clawed to reach its sick of sin.
Despair it raged inside these walls, left malls and churches sallow halls.
But deft of spirit, soldiered on, the ones who woke to new birds' song.

They sensed their chance to rise anew, the tremor rippled deeply through
the streets and roads, the fields and hills, the pastures green, satanic mills…
Until a swell at last was reached, that saw us fight them on the beach.

The hope eternal swelled once more and tapped its fingers on the door,
of every house, in every street,
that knew not others' near defeat.
It came defiant - rally call,
as one, and two, and more walked tall.
The knowing that the chance was here
for untouched bodies, baring near
to once again embrace the dear.

As joined arms led and lent and loved, the shared, cared fellows back for good.
For good, this time, pray, let it be – that war is over finally.

Harmony

Phil Saunders

1
we could be driven/kept apart
by strangeness.

so what collects us
together
as more than strangers in the neighbourhood?

the smile in each other's eyes
the welcome in each other's attitude
the delight in each other's offerings
that drive this community
we call home.

a strangeness/strangers
no longer
regardless of
the tone of skin
the food we eat
the clothes we wear
the language we speak
the culture we practice

2
we were all strangers
once.

when we mouth the words
respect
acceptance
inclusiveness
and mean them,
when we say
hello
welcome
how are you
join us,
we are strangers no more.

Opposites

Miles Hitchcock

Any phenomenon that believes it governs
the forces around it
will find collision.

Any nation or conversation
that tries to hold sway
will end in conflict.

Any endeavor
social, political, artistic, scientific
that forms barriers
will meet resistance.

Any charity or compassion
that draws lines in the sand
will dissolve.

Any being that doesn't put itself in the way
of its opposite
but flows around it
preserves itself.

Away Forward

Phil Saunders

Away
Away
For escape from sorrow
For adventure in love
For toil and play
To move beyond
Leaving everything / and nothing
To be different / and the same
An ancient rhythm
The essence of who we are.

Hello In Any Language Is Just Hello
Bryan Franco

Hola Aloha Shalom
They all look alike.
Hola Aloha Shalom.
They even sound alike.
Hola Aloha Shalom.
Words of different languages
with no cultural connection
to each other
From places in the world
considered to be
far reaches
from each other
Said by people
whose languages
that are so different,
they should not
be able
to figure out
anything
the others say.
But every language
has a hello
that can greet
anyone in the world.

Hola Aloha Shalom.
They all look alike.
They even sound alike.
They are words
that might point to people
who practice the lost art of courtesy,
People who say please
and thank you
and you're welcome
on a regular basis,
People who others
call kind and well-mannered,
a potential subset
of groups of others.
But not an other

if everyone took
the truly little time
it takes
to be courteous and kind,
maybe by learning words
from other languages
like Hola, Aloha, and Shalom,
we can learn
that being a human being
is something
everyone everywhere
cannot avoid being,
potentially eliminating
the need
to refer
to another human being
as other.

Globalisation
Una Lappin

G is for the GLOBE that we all love and share
L is for the LEARNING that we all do to care,

O is for the OCEANS that keep us all apart
B is for the BORDERS that are now an open heart,

A is for the ACKNOWLEDGEMENT that we all now work smart
L is for the LIST of time-zones we keep on a chart,

I is for the INTENTIONS that we all set and weave
S is for the SATISFACTION that we all get when we achieve,

A is for the APPETITE that we all don't want to lose
T is for the TECHNOLOGY that we now all overuse,

I is for the INTERNET that we would all not cope without
O is for the OPPORTUNITIES that we all shout about,

N is for the NOW that we all find ourselves in,
... Which is a more connected world where we all now live in.

Space Station Passing Over Our House In West Preston

Stephen Smithyman

Tipped off by our space photographer nephew,
we stand out on our suburban street
at a quarter-to-ten at night to see the space station
cross the enormous sky above our tiny
corner of the world. With our binoculars, we search
the sky, desperate for a glimpse. First
we think it might be Venus, shining brightly above
the dark pines of the cemetery at the end
of the street – love triumphing over death, after all...
Suddenly, we see it, a travelling light, high up
in the dome of the sky, moving with surprising speed
and certainty along its pre-ordained path
towards its goal – the far-distant horizon – where
it vanishes from sight. It orbits the earth
once every ninety minutes, they say, nimbly threading
its way between asteroids and satellites –
the general litter of space debris – a fragile container
of hope, symbol of faith in a united, off-world,
high-tech future, while we turn and walk slowly back
to our house in the divided, declining world below.

Global Eyes

Eleanor May Blackburn

The edge of the earth
Is like
The edge of your crooked smile
I could drop off either one
And fall
Fall
Fall
Into nothingness
Until eventually
I land soft and firm
With a single bounce
Carried by a sea
Of different shades and sizes
Of fingers and thumbs
In line with blinking lids
All ready
To push me upwards
Like the hands in the film
Labyrinth
Facing towards a familiar destination
A combined hypothetical location
All connected through distant
But deep rooted
Relation
We are bonded by a seam that is bright
That seam is united

Regenesis

Anne Casey

If ever you find yourself
in a place of unusual incongruity,
at odds with someone, something
or other, the whole universe, or even
just yourself,
take the time
to remember
when everything was grey
and all over the world
people were dying
of one thing
or another
(but mostly that one thing)
—a disappearing as if
into an abyss:
a great grey abscess
which was an absence
and how: when it became clear,
a wave, small at first
then swelling to a
tremendous roar
filled the whole world
with the understanding
and that was called
the end of times
because after it
came the beginning:
and the world
was made new,
filled
with that
essential
that had
once been

so greatly
missing

if only we had realised
sooner

Tin Roof
Hiram Larew

When I was 17
        apples were busheled in baskets
        and I was the straw under all of those red round spirits.
All the light coming in
        was planked and slanted across them
        and every wasp in the world
        hovered just above them.
Yes
Whatever apples were
        I wanted to be.

And in a way
        when I was 17
        apples ate me --
What was to become my heart
        was only some wild weedy row in the orchard back then.
And any sheen reflecting off their skins or the barn's tin roof
        was all that I wanted to be.

When I was 17
        with every seed buried deep inside
        even my gangly gaze was humming.
And somehow I knew before tasting anything
        tartly sweet
        that that was what I wanted to be
        right there
        in the baskets.

Ceasefire
Geoffrey Aitken

History
documents
global
human interaction
records efforts
to maintain
equilibrium
with negotiated
peace agreements
pacts
plans
but
even unread
children know

love
is unconditional

Identities

Miles Hitchcock

Race gender class
ethnicity, ideology
all these things called identities
are just predicaments.

Predicaments are there to be overcome.
Life grows out of itself
adding previous numbers into an expanding curve
and the only way to transcend
is to include.

The cell transcends the genome.
The body transcends the cell.
Earth carries its species
through a solar garden.
All have momentum, position, a singular fate:
all identities grow from a previous state.

If you want to know a person's predicament
listen to what they say, every day.

If you want to see a person,
look into their eyes.

You will see the same light
that shines from yours.

The Magic Within

Gerard Traub

Let the workings of every machine
fade in lustre
echoes of antiquated motion
beyond the inventions of fire and wheel
the atom splitting nations
and humanity agape
soon nature to intercede.

Through walls of other worlds
many cries can be heard
with heart calling from the bodice
of blinding technologies
sustaining our widened
and weary search.

Illuminate our ways and becomings
until all fossils are fuel no more
truth remember your flame
terror finding its conquests
closing now on strident shores.

The magic within us
dims every machine
here to follow untold frontiers.

Clatter
Hiram Larew

Love me in the very same way that the word *unbeknownst* sounds
in midair
Yes
or just like how spires climb to the very top
And then even beyond soap's slip or noon's drift
and as far as puddles can jump
Love to love me like that

And love me as if handshakes were grins
or as when echoes find their tunnel
Love me like those birds that love diving and corners
or just like sunlight is love
as it teases the cupboards
Love me in all those ways and more

And with sashes open
Love me now but also then
and as much as when
lunch is served
with all of that back and forth and clatter
Yes love me as surely as cups that will spill

Or then above
with night's excel
when listening turns to dreams
Love me like the swirling din
within the word *abound*

Influence Of Moon

Dr. Deidra Suwanee Dees

like the lonely moon
silent
          motionless,

standing still
in time

the way I feel
despite

          globalisation
of my history,

disconnected

separate
          from Creator

          broken,
          alone

all alone,

at the lonely moon
I gaze

silent
brilliant,

eyes are
watching,

to her Creator
I pray

illumination
exhalation

relentless
light

recaptured brilliance

by earthlings

Great Migrations
Daragh Byrne

Arctic tern live the two-summers dream
at the cost of the longest known round-trip.
Two dozen times or more they'll wing it
in a lifespan, almost twenty thousand
mile each way. Every migration is an act
of ferocious focus; a bird in transit will
refuse an offered herring that a local gull
will devour. A straight-line gamble that declares
I can eat later; leave me to my purpose. There is
mating and hatching; the vicissitudes of
nesting, and feeding, all of which are foreplay
for the compulsion of return.
In Abu Dhabi
airport — my least favourite — it isn't easy
to resist the overpriced pastries and jetlag
strength coffee proffered at each corner,
but my route is direct, and my intention is
clear. A couple beside me wrestle their
children; I'm glad I fly solo, though I have to
put aside a midnight flicker of worry —
there is no need for me to be *for* anything,
in that way. I watch, and I write things down,
and from time to time I find my way home.

Resolution
Heather Barker Vermeer

To the brave ones,
the enslaved
ones,
the ones who've lost
their
way.
The flying high,
four-car guy
who never has to pay.

The anxious girl
The Fucked Up World,
the glorified,
the gay.
The non-descript, front-tooth chipped, pissed up
every day.
The photoshopped,
the breast lift opped,
the tanned,
the pale,
the grey.
The thread-veined, cling film wrinkled hands
that fought
and held
and prayed…

The empaths and the egos,
the cleaners short on pay,
the top floor corner office bloke,
euphoric kids at play.

Strong in our voices,
firm in our truths,
togetherness - our way.

We'll laugh,
We'll dance,
We'll share,
We'll sing:
"Love them all!"
today.

This Small World

D.L. Lang

The world is now a melting pot
more so than ever before.
You can have a pen pal from Siberia,
learn about every culture and faith,
order artwork straight from India,
or dine on delicacies from Berlin.
The more we learn about each other
the better off this world will be,
for once we celebrate our differences,
we shall learn to live in harmony.
Perhaps, the more we stay connected,
we'll figure out a grand new plan
to protect our earth from harm,
eradicating hunger, war and poverty,
and bringing blessings to every human.
We have such a long way to go,
but every day brings us closer,
and we can never let go of hope,
so come on, let us all join hands.

Global Citizen
Nathalie Sallegren

A loaded gun asks her: Where do you belong?

3rd culture kid. Now there's a label that fits… sort of.
A person raised in a culture other than their own or the one named on their passport.
Change management expert, A community covert.
International chameleon; Dyslexic in origin,

Packed full of traditions lost Entangled in conditions tossed
In my repetitive incessant culture shock.
Cultivated by a hardcore feminist matriarch
With her past left in the dark farmyards near the vineyards of Southern France.
Rounded out by a kind-hearted father who defied his own destiny
leaving coal mine industry of soot ridden England. Sought to fill curiosity.

Bouncing from continent Europe to Melanesia, Australasia and back again
My mother tongue twice removed, is fading away again
My second language gave way, distorted by the wretched dregs of Aussie rednecks
My third languages 1 & 2 Pigeon English and Motu, gone but for the handful of go to-s
Finnish and now Swedish have me craving my origins

I fit nowhere and everywhere simultaneously as I'm saying, see…
I'd love to explain to you about the dislocated sensation of acculturation in my impending modification to the next location, but I think you might get jealous. Need to belong seems to penetrate my motivation for assimilation.
Schools up to here. Some of which helped me, most of which shaped me to see what not to be.
Self-esteem plummeting as no school system really fit me. Alien.
It's ok though if I think of myself as a fish on a bicycle,
where the imagery ironical, maintains my confidential, which gave me soul sensational.

Water rises in pools I swam in at the footstep of my home now drownin',
Corrupt systemic pollutants repel me from the corners I used to hide in.
Third world existence flail against first world betrayals in the shrill
vast hearts of the bastards that bask in their own good fortune.

Waterfalls surround and beat down around me

Boom rush of memories exhilarate my freedom
Suns glance seizes me
Dancing droplets leap up and greet me
Crystal rapids giggle and tease me

Liberty suspended atmospherically

I look down on the puddle that has been such a muddle of vast open oceans
Of distant commotions

and my passport now gleams from opportunity
it depends how you look at it
International citizen

So, when I ask you Where are you from?
I don't mean, where do you belong?
I mean what shaped you ... What makes you?
How did you become the being that you are and where do your hopes take you?

Dwelling

C.Creative

My heart dwells in a time
where castles are comforted by overlapping and twisted vines
Where I find myself walking
through a mysterious mist on a rocky pathway that is signature
to my soul and leads to home
Handwritten love letters delivered by a messenger
that I had yearned months upon for

The thrill of your hands, one holding mine
The other resting on my begging spine
Our shadows dancing beneath us
Portraits burning my mind of your eyes that hold a thousand
Un-lived love stories, locked in with mine being held and treasured in
the safest parts of my mind

Awaiting our next encounter with skin that mourns your slightest touch your
slightest movement in any direction

My heart dwells in a time
When poetry wasn't poetry at all,
but simply a magnificent way to love and live

Littorally

Devika Brendon

The way the ocean withdrew that day
Reminds me of so much that has happened since
It was not the way things ought to be
A strange and surreal counterpoint:
A true crime without evidence.

Now we are on the littoral
Sitting on the edge of that fiery fence
The dry stone wall between us
And here it comes, the huge wave, the love
Roaring into the space
carved by its absence.

Poetry Is
Kimberly Johnson

Poetry is the way a woman snuggles
        into the spoon of her lover's embrace while she sleeps.
It's the darkness that surrounds her,
    though she be in a room full of people.
Poetry is oxygen- sustaining life; a releasing of carbon dioxide,
        its words flowing free- healing the damage
        and destruction of all the toxins she's been swallowing.
It's the cure to what ails you- minus visits to the doctor,
    copays and time wasted.
Poetry is a road not paved in hate.
It is goodness and mercy. It is grace.
A table prepared before thine enemies.
Poetry is fluid. A never-ending motion.
It's depths deeper than any ocean.
Poetry can handle all of this emotion.
It is love. It is anger.
It is the green monster, the one eyed one horned purple people eater.
Poetry is the ability to believe one eyed one horned purple eaters do exist.

Poetry is this-
A sweet blessedness that can't be taken away
        regardless of what people have to say.
It is night turning into day, knowing mourning won't last always.
Dreariness, clouds, tears and rain will fade, but poetry remains.
It is a safety net as you trapeze across the sky,
        daring you to explore limits beyond what you can see.
Poetry is always asking why and never satisfied
        with the cautionary tales of others.
Poetry is a mother, rocking you to sleep,
        encouraging you to make your dreams reality.
Poetry is a father. Damn.
Maybe that's something we don't always see
        or perhaps it's a gift taken way to soon-

Walls

Ian Cameron Wood

globalisation?
the removal of boundaries? removal of borders?
removal of what separates us from each other?
removal of the cultural divide?
removal of class differences?
removal of poverty, removal of starvation?
removal of climate change?
removal of terrorists? removal of war?

but we cannot remove our enemies who
also want to remove their enemies,
we are like them, they are like us,
we are them, they are us.

globalisation means those of other races are ourselves,
those of other religions are ourselves,
those of other nations are ourselves,
the rich and the poor are ourselves,
the weak and the strong are ourselves,
the healthy and the ailing are ourselves,
those who are different are ourselves.

those who promise a better tomorrow are ourselves,
those who threaten us with doom are ourselves.

those who build walls are ourselves.

jericho built walls to keep out the israelites,
but the walls fell, and jericho was destroyed – localisation?
masada built walls to keep the romans out
but those within died at their own hands – nationalisation?
hadrian built a wall to keep the picts and scots in,
but the romans marched away – colonisation?
east germany built a wall to keep the west out,
but that wall was pulled down by ourselves – globalisation?

those across the borders are ourselves,
those across the boundaries are ourselves,
those across the seas are ourselves,
those across the mountains are ourselves,
those across the country are ourselves,
those across town are ourselves,
those across the street are ourselves.

but, we are all still behind the wall.

The Sphere Keeps Spinning
Kelly Van Nelson

We have fallen into the abyss
of a materialistic dream
where we forgot to be lean and green
and our own needs and greed
eclipsed those of the planet
we needed to feed and norish.

Tomorrow we will be gone
to another place beyond here
where nothing is familiar
and the life we once knew
is just another turned page in history.

Our mortal bodies will be still
in the darkness beneath the earth
while Mother Nature
continues doing her work
to keep the sphere spinning another day.

KELLY VAN NELSON

Kelly Van Nelson is a contemporary author, poet, and spoken word artist from Newcastle-upon-Tyne, now living in Australia. Her poems, short stories, and non-fiction articles have featured in numerous international publications and she regularly appears on radio and television discussing current issues prevalent in society. Several of her poetry movies have streamed at literary festivals and she is the co-curator and co-host of Wordsmith: A Poetry Podcast. She is represented by The Newman Agency.

Graffiti Lane, her powerful debut poetry collection, showcased at the London Book Fair and became an instant bestseller, raising awareness and influencing change around bullying, mental health, and suicide. *Punch and Judy*, her second #1 bestselling poetry collection, puts the spotlight on domestic violence, generating much needed conversation. She is also the author of *Rolling in the Mud: A Short Story Collection.* Her books have been gifted to television celebrities, music icons, and A-List Hollywood Oscar nominees and winners.

Kelly is a KSP First Edition Fellowship recipient, an Aus-Mumpreneur 'Big Idea - Changing the World' Gold Award winner for her creative use of the literary word as an antibullying advocate, a double Roar Success Award winner for Best Book (Graffiti Lane) and Most Powerful Influencer, Roar Success Silver Award winner for Social Media Star and the Bronze winner of the Making A Difference Award. She is also a 2020 Telstra Business Women's Award and CEO Magazine Managing Director of the Year Finalist.

Kelly is the mum of two children, wife of her soulmate of more than two decades and Managing Director on the executive board of a Fortune 500. In the spare time she doesn't have, you can find her hanging out on the open mic performing slam poetry or fusing poetry with film. In short, she is a juggler.

www.kellyvannelson.com

THANK YOU TO THE FOLLOWING CONTRIBUTING POETS

Geoffrey Aitken's poetry is published in "New Poets 19", & in print/ online AUS, US, UK, Fr and CAN, where his minimalist industrial signature appeals. He is concerned about avenue life mental health.

Imogen Arate is an award-winning Asian-American poet and the Host of Poets and Muses, an award-winning weekly poetry podcast. Her work was recently featured in The New Verse News and dyst Journal. Global geopolitics and the ways in which they affect people's interaction in daily life are of enormous interest to her.

Western Australia based artist (performing and writer), Yola Bakker not only works in creative ways in the mining industry, she is a thought-leader who challenges paradigms and people.

Eleanor May Blackburn is an actor and writer from England. She has most recently been writing and performing her own spoken word which has been featured on the local radio station and acting in many short films.

Devika Brendon is a writer, teacher, editor and reviewer of English Language and Literature. She is the Senior Content Editor of the literary journal, New Ceylon Writing, established in 1970, and brought online in 2016. Devika's short stories and poetry have been internationally published in anthologies and journals, including Quadrant Magazine, and her reviews have been published in Australia, India and Sri Lanka. Devika is a newspaper columnist in Sri Lanka, and her articles and opinion pieces are published in Ceylon Today, The Sunday Island, The Sunday Times and LMD Magazine.

Trevor Burndred is a poet and writer who experiments with different styles, often embracing his passion for music. He is inspired by subjects everywhere; nature, the environment, social issues, pets, people, and the most natural thing for a poet … love and romance.

Caroline Burrows is a writer of poetry, and fiction. Her most recent commission '#PoetryHelps: Suicide Awareness & Prevention' was for Glenside Hospital Museum with Bristol Festival of Ideas.

Daragh Byrne is an Irish poet living and writing in Sydney, Australia. He is currently Convener of The Sydney Poetry Lounge, a longstanding open mic night.

Rosa Caraffa is an author and publisher of her own press. Her genre relates to life happenings, in particular to loss, death and the grieving process. Her life message is 'Never give up on Hope'.

Anne Casey is an award-winning Irish poet/writer living in Australia, widely published internationally. She is a journalist, magazine editor, legal author & media communications director for 30 years.

Megan Chapman is a writer whose lifetime of metaphysical study has her always looking for the deeper meaning. Words are her tools to articulate what she finds in her soul. Poetry is her catharsis.

Michael Collins from Newcastle, NSW: Teacher; Nurse, Support Worker. Born in 1954. Likes Zoom events, and Poetry At The Pub. Retired. Reads as much as possible... Building a cabin in the woods... (In my backyard)

Angela Costi is the author of 4 poetry collections including Honey and Salt (Five Islands Press 2007) and Lost in Mid-Verse (Owl Publishing 2014). Recent poems are in Otoliths, Writers Resist, APJ.

Jeff Cottrill is a journalist, fiction writer, and poet in Toronto, Canada. He has headlined in countless literary series throughout Canada and the U.K. Jeff is currently working on his first novel.

Bryan Franco lives in Brunswick, Maine USA. He likes writing poetry and occasionally reading it in front of anyone who'll listen. He is a painter, sculptor, master gardener, and culinary genius.

Margaret Frodsham is a poet from Perth, Western Australia. Her pen name is Margaret Harcourt West and she has written two children's books: 'Flying Santa' and 'Winifred the Wonder Witch.' Both books are available on Google and many other sites.

Chelsea Green (C.Creative) is a young mother with an old soul, from Perth, Western Australia. Being adopted as a baby she spent a lot of her life confused, always searching, writing to help articulate things she couldn't express in any other way. Her first book of poetry is called "Collateral Beauty".

Fraser Gordon describes himself as a natural misanthrope with a penchant for occasional bouts of controlled frivolity. He enjoys reading fiction despite acknowledging the world is quite strange enough as it is. He likes writing poetry, outdoorsy things, squirrels, and his knees. His inspiration for poetry comes from having lived at times, a very strange life. He tries to see the good in people and works very hard at being the best version of himself so that his wife will continue to suffer under the illusion that he's worth keeping around.

Fin Hall has been pretending to be a poet for around 50 years. He knew he had made it when he was published in Sounds Music Paper in 1972, then about 20 years later another one was included in 'Voices in the wind' anthology. He is now on a roll with several pieces in online publications and in printed books. He curates Joined Up Writing, an ongoing collaborative work and is the host of 'Like A Blot From The Blue Zoom Show'.

Julia Kaylock is a poet, writer, editor and artist based on the Mornington Peninsula in Victoria, Australia. Her work has been published in a wide range of online and print literary journals and anthologies including The Blue Nib (Issue 49, 2020) and Grieve (Hunter Writers' Centre, 2020). Julia is the editor of several anthologies including Messages from the Embers: From Devastation to Hope (Black Quill Press, 2020) and Poetry for the Planet: An Anthology of Imagined Futures (in production). She is currently finalising her memoir in verse, Child of the Clouds to be published under her imprint, Litoria Press.

Miles Hitchcock is a writer, teacher and musician living in Perth, WA. He has previously won the Melbourne Age Short Story Award, and the Curtin Fiction Prize.

Dane Ince published in Lit Today, Journal of Expressive Writing, Haiku Action, Pendemic Journal. Dane traveled from his place of birth in Texas to Berkeley, California to study art.

Lindy Jelliman is a lover of words to inspire action in important areas including mental health. She is the author of "Tinker Tailor's Toolbox (For Mending Broken Hearts)" - a mental health resource for kids.

Kimberly Johnson is a poet from Richmond, Virginia, USA. Under the name Kimberly Jay, she's wrote Journey to Forgiveness and contributed to several anthologies. She is also a spoken word artist, known as Special K, engaging audiences with word-spiration not soon be forgotten.

Gerald Kells performs poetry around Walsall, the English Midlands and the Internet. His YouTube Channel is full of amusing and serious goodies and his collection, 51 Poems, is available online.

Franchesa Kirkpatrick is a Nashville, Tennessee native and full time creative. She is a regular on the Zoom Poetry circuit worldwide and is always looking for more adventures to experience and to write about.

Una Lappin is the founder of Unique New Adventure, delivering workshops/talks/storytelling from lived humanitarian experiences from continents Asia and Africa. She is a published author in The Business of Connection's Anthology.

D.L. Lang served as Poet Laureate of Vallejo, California (2017-2019). Her work also appears in Colossus: Home, A Poet's Siddur, and on ReformJudaism.org She can be found online at poetryebook.com.

Claire Language is a 21-year-old poet. She is a constant emotional mess.

Hiram Larew's Poetry X Hunger initiative is bring poets from around the world to the anti-hunger cause – https://www.PoetryXHunger.com/

Mike Mackay is a new author and poet to watch out for. He has a Masters's degree in Computer Science and has spent decades implementing Enterprise-Level business systems into corporates around the world. This work led him to uncover 'the evil that men do' in the business world. Getting to do forensic work has been by word of mouth. He is also actively involved in martial arts. Mike lives in Perth, Western Australia.

Des Mannay's first poetry collection, "Sod 'em – and tomorrow" was published by Waterloo Press. He is co-editor of The Angry Manifesto poetry journal and has placed in five and shortlisted in seven literary competitions. His work has appeared in twenty poetry anthologies.

Denise O'Hagan has a background in commercial book publishing and is Poetry Editor for Australia/New Zealand for The Blue Nib. Her poetry is published widely and has received numerous awards.

Maroulla Radisavic is a part-time Greek teacher. She studied Social Sciences in Prague Czech. She writes poetry, children's stories and memoirs. She loves translating, arts, textiles and the Greek Mythology.

Riya Rajesh is passionate about voicing her experiences as a young, brown woman in Melbourne; through writing, spoken word and community event management. Check out her Instagram @ riyawritesincolour.

Nathalie Sallegren is currently living in Finland. She is an Australian performance poet from WA & the Red Centre, British born, French origin, Papua New Guinean raised. Nathalie's themes examine globalization and isolation in connection.

Phil Saunders is a wordsmith professionally and personally as a copy writer, policy officer, magazine and report editor and poet, published in hard copy and online journals and played on ABC radio.

Stephen Smithyman is a retired school-teacher, living in Melbourne. 'Space Station Over Our House' is taken from his new collection, 'Halfway and Back' (Ginninderra Press, Adelaide, 2020).

Dr. Deidra Suwanee Dees is Director/Tribal Archivist at Poarch Band of Creek Indians. She earned her doctorate at Harvard, writing about the Indigenous experience in Muscogee Education Movement. Her poetry in this collection represents globalisation and is taken from her poetry manuscript, "Indian Ice: Indigenous Witness". Heleswv heres, Mvto.

Kristy-Lee Swift is an Author, Freelance writer and Editor on the Mornington Peninsula, Victoria. As a busy mother of two young girls she is an active performance poet and all-round life juggler.

Markey Mark Symmonds is an English poet and writer who regularly performs at open mic events and more recently via zoom. His work has been published in three anthologies and several online magazines. He writes and performs free verse on anything from politics to love and anything that pops into his head at 3am in the morning.

Gerard Traub lives with his family on the Sunshine Coast, Queensland. He is the author of a collection of poetry "Reflections of Nature", and a children's book "Lily the Lotus".

Glenda Traub is inspired by the creative arts. She enjoys the beauty of nature, and is passionate about the preservation of the natural environment and all its inhabitants.

Kayin Van Nelson is a seventeen-year-old emerging film director and creative writer. He is the winner of the SHC Young Filmmaker Award and 1st place Write for Fun short story prize winner. He completed a film director course at AFTRS and a one-year scriptwriting course at KSP Writers Centre. He has had short stories and poetry published and has directed, edited, and composed music for short films, live shows, author launches and spoken word events, with film reels screened at Melbourne Fringe and Melbourne Spoken Word Festival.

Through humaninterest.co.nz Heather Barker Vermeer enables people and businesses to share their 'essence in ink'. She is a writer and former magazine editor with a BA in Linguistics and English Language and a journalism post-grad.

Susan Wakefield is a distinguished Freelance Writer, Novelist, Editor and published Poet returning to Australia after twenty years in The United States and France, now writing her 6th novel, Decency.

Toni Wass has always been a writer and a poet. From the first short story in English class at school, to a novel about an Australian War Bride; to a self-published book of poems. It's in the DNA.

Skylar J Wynter, winner of the 2020 KSP Unpublished Author Program is celebrating the recent launch of her first book, Pieces of Humanity. A writer of poetry and fiction and addicted to Zoom open mic.

Marianne Murphy Zarzana, and her husband, sci-fi author James A. Zarzana, live in South Bend, Indiana. They love to travel, especially to Sweden to visit family. www.mariannezarzana.com

Ian Cameron Wood is a newly published author. His first book *Hidden in the Light* was published in January 2021 by MMH Press.

www.ingramcontent.com/pod-product-compliance
Lightning Source LLC
Chambersburg PA
CBHW021952290426
44108CB00012B/1038
9780645096613